The Illustrated Book of

BASIC
BOATING

The Illustrated Book of

BASIC
BOATING

By Christopher Caswell

*Illustrated by James E. Mitchell and
Lawrence J. Zwart*

Hearst Marine Books
New York

This book is exactly what its title implies, an illustrated guide to basic boating, not a textbook meant to replace manufacturer manuals, basic boating courses or applicable government publications. The publisher and the author urge readers to become certified for basic boating through accredited boating organizations and not to use this book as a substitute.

It is the policy of William Morrow and Company, Inc., and its imprints and affiliates, recognizing the importance of preserving what has been written, to print the books we publish on acid-free paper, and we exert our best efforts to that end.

Library of Congress Catalog Card Number: 89-81523
ISBN: 0-688-08931-3

Printed in the United States of America

45678910

Contents

Chapter 1

Welcome Aboard

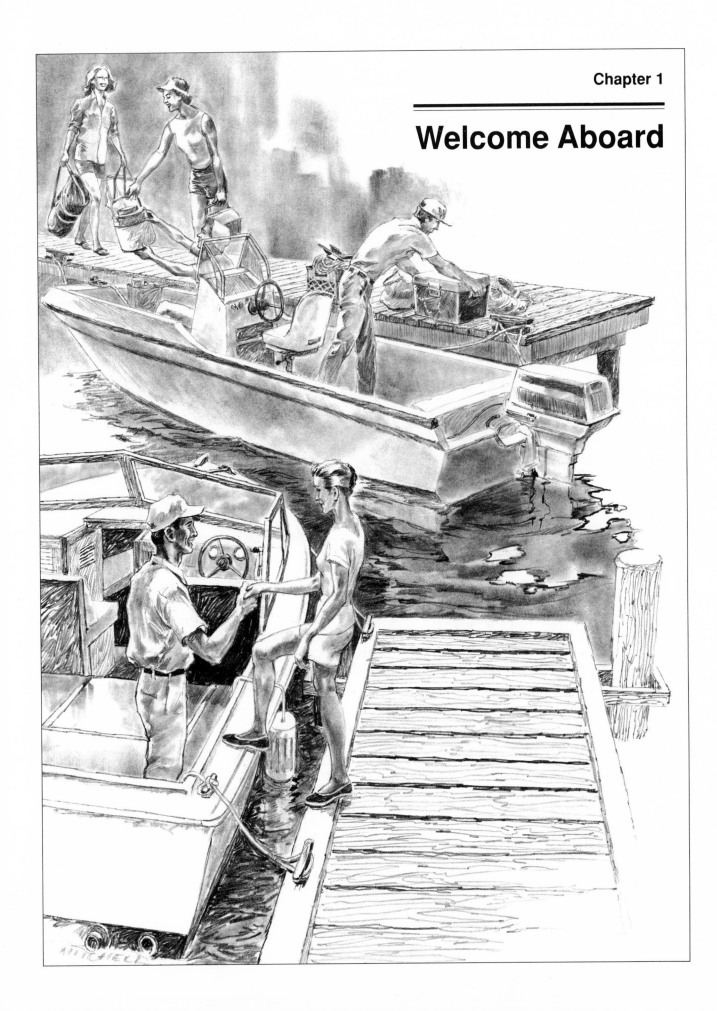

Waterborne Activities

Simply being out on the water is enough for some people. For others, of course, boating is synonymous with special activities such as waterskiing, fishing, cruising, beachcombing, picnicking, swimming, even camping. Your choice of waterborne activity will determine the kind of boat you select and the body of water you use it on, but any of these activities can be enjoyed in a 15- to 30-foot powerboat.

Day Cruising: Much like going for an afternoon drive in your car, day cruises offer variety ranging from exploring a bustling port to enjoying a secluded river. Unlike a car, however, a boat provides a means of getting to out-of-the-way places accessible only by water.

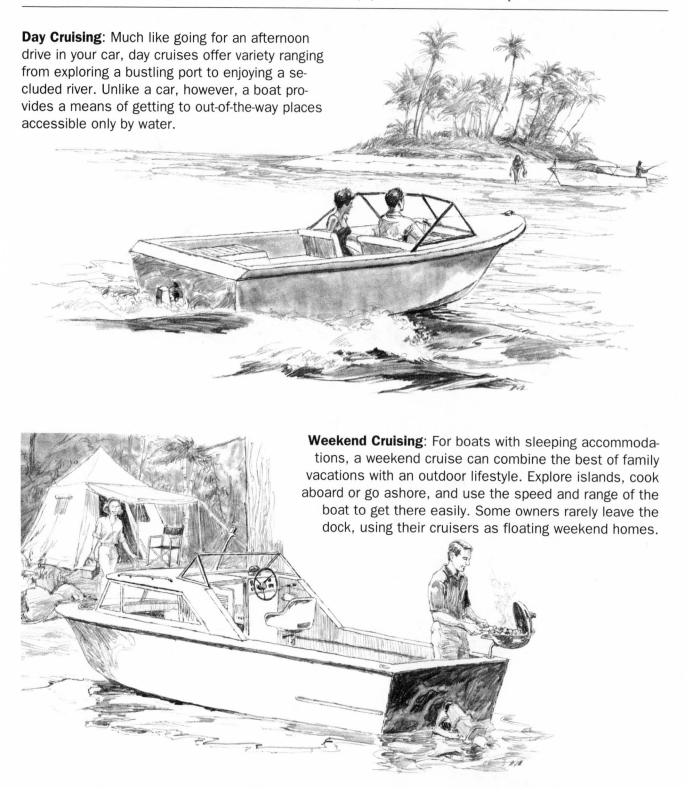

Weekend Cruising: For boats with sleeping accommodations, a weekend cruise can combine the best of family vacations with an outdoor lifestyle. Explore islands, cook aboard or go ashore, and use the speed and range of the boat to get there easily. Some owners rarely leave the dock, using their cruisers as floating weekend homes.

When you first enter the world of boating, you may have no specific interest in mind. But as your experience grows, you are apt to explore fresh activities. Many boatowners find that they have discovered entire new worlds they would never have guessed could bring them so much enjoyment. For others, merely getting out onto the water and away from it all is sufficient incentive to buy a boat.

Fishing: The most popular use for a powerboat, fishing can take you from familiar local grounds to offshore fishing areas. Trolling at low speed, drifting or anchored, a powerboat is the perfect platform for catching dinner.

Waterskiing: One of the fastest growing sports in the nation, waterskiing is healthy, challenging and fun. Many locations have designated waterskiing areas. Some states require an observer for safety reasons.

Skindiving: The familiar red and white "diver down" flag indicates that skindivers are in the area, exploring a wreck or catching lobster for dinner. Powerboats can carry a full load of tanks, gear and divers to new waters every weekend.

Basic Terminology

Newcomers often find marine terms foreign and confusing. Nautical language, however, is used as a shorthand for referring to objects found nowhere else but on boats and on the water. Mastering basic terms will help you make yourself clear quickly when issuing commands since marine terms are precise and thus reduce confusion.

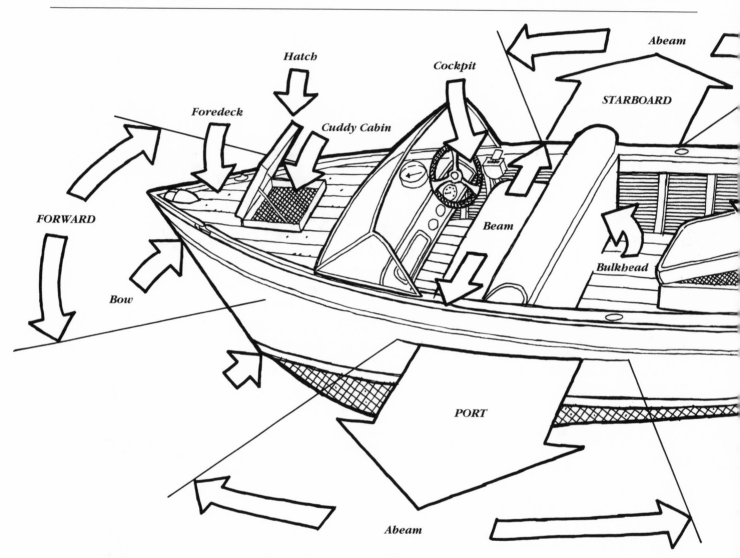

DIRECTIONS AND BASIC BOAT TERMS

Abeam: At right angles to a boat

Aft: Toward the stern

Beam: The widest point of a boat

Bow: The forwardmost part of a boat

Bulkhead: A vertical wall in a boat

Cockpit: A recessed area where the crew sits

Cuddy/Cabin: An enclosed living and storage area located under the forward deck

Deck: Floor or flooring

Foredeck: The covered deck area at the bow

Forward: Toward the bow

Freeboard: The vertical distance between the waterline and the deck

Hatch: An opening in a deck or bulkhead

Port: The left side of the boat when facing forward

Starboard: The right side of the boat when facing forward

Stern: The back part of the boat

Transom: The outer surface of the stern, or the entire stern panel

Waterline: The line around the hull that marks where the boat floats at rest

Like learning a foreign language, terminology is easiest to remember through frequent and repeated use. Make it a point to use the proper word while aboard your boat (and have your crew do the same). It won't be long before using marine terms feels comfortable. You'll also find that knowing the terms makes reading boating magazines and new boat brochures easier, more instructive and more enjoyable.

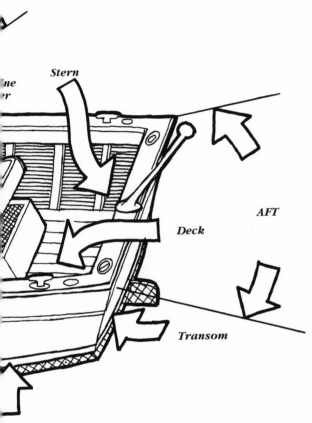

SYSTEM TERMS
Anchor Light: A white light displayed at night while the boat is anchored
Bilge Blower: A Coast Guard-required electrically operated fan for supplying fresh air to and exhausting fumes from the engine compartment
Bowrail: A grabrail around the front of the boat
Capacity Plate: A required plate that displays maximum capacities and horsepower for a boat
Control Panel: The instrument panel on a boat
Engine Cover: An enclosure over the engine on an inboard or sterndrive boat
Fuel Filler: The opening in the deck that leads to the gas tank, closed with a screw-on cap
Fuel Line: The metal or rubber hose that carries fuel to the engine from the tank
Gearshift/Throttle: Controls for speed and direction
Head: A marine toilet
Helm: The steering wheel
Horn: Used to warn others of your presence and to signal your intentions to other boats
Navigation Lights: Lights required for night operation
Outdrive: The propulsion unit for a sterndrive boat
Prop: The propeller
Rubrail: A metal or rubber railing around the deck that protects the hull
Stern Light: A white navigation light mounted at the stern of a boat for night operation

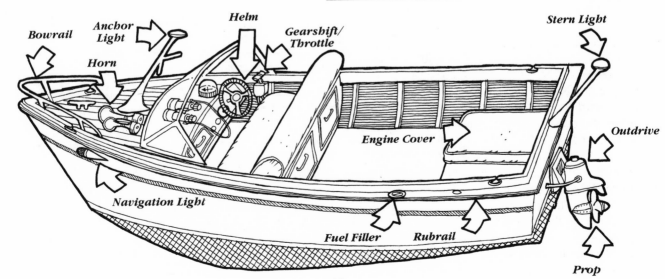

Basic Terminology

Learning nautical language can be frustrating. Why not simply say left and right instead of port and starboard? Because right and left are directions relative to where you happen to be facing at the moment, whereas the port and starboard sides of a boat don't change, regardless of where you are facing. In an emergency, time is saved when you use the proper word.

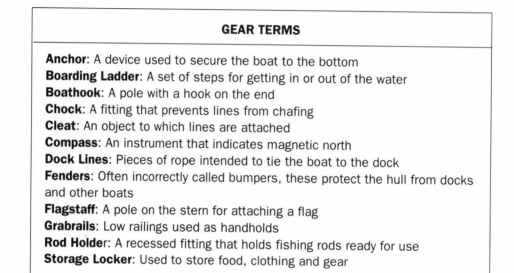

GEAR TERMS

Anchor: A device used to secure the boat to the bottom
Boarding Ladder: A set of steps for getting in or out of the water
Boathook: A pole with a hook on the end
Chock: A fitting that prevents lines from chafing
Cleat: An object to which lines are attached
Compass: An instrument that indicates magnetic north
Dock Lines: Pieces of rope intended to tie the boat to the dock
Fenders: Often incorrectly called bumpers, these protect the hull from docks and other boats
Flagstaff: A pole on the stern for attaching a flag
Grabrails: Low railings used as handholds
Rod Holder: A recessed fitting that holds fishing rods ready for use
Storage Locker: Used to store food, clothing and gear

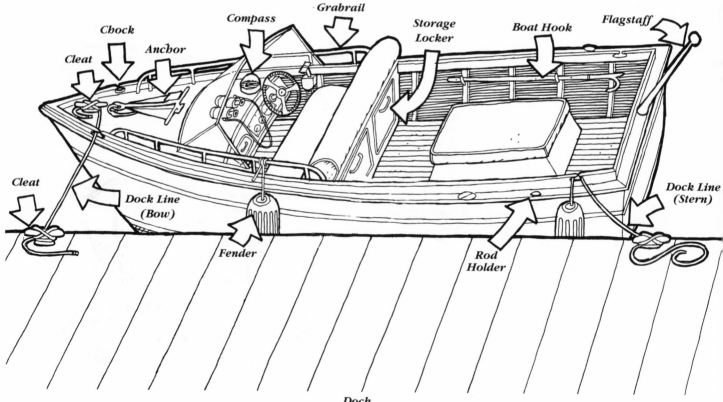

Boat Hull Types

For many years, hull design was dictated by the shapes wood could assume. With the advent of fiberglass, however, designers have been free to develop new hull types that provide better riding qualities, higher speeds and superior seaworthiness. While the flat-bottomed design is still found in skiffs and rowboats, most modern powerboats are either deep-V, modified deep-V or tri-hulled in shape.

Deep-V: This hull is essentially wedge-shaped from the bow to the stern. Strakes, small horizontal strips added below the waterline, serve to lift the hull up out of the water at speed as well as to push spray out to the sides. The deep-V hull is the smoothest riding hull in choppy conditions since it softens the pounding from waves. As a result, the design is used for offshore powerboat racing and many builders have adapted it to family runabouts. The drawback to deep-Vs is that they tend to roll at low speeds or at rest in choppy conditions.

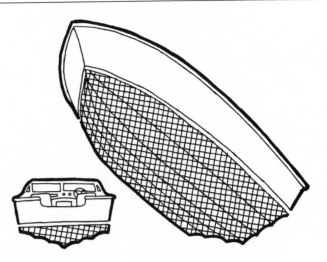

Modified Deep-V: This is the hull you're most likely to encounter in a modern powerboat since it combines some of the best characteristics of other shapes. Like the deep-V, it is extremely wedge-shaped in the forward area but it flattens out near the stern to a flatter V-shape. At speed, the deep-V forward helps to cushion the ride and push the spray aside. The flatter area under the stern provides more stability at low speeds and, in smooth water, helps increase speed by allowing the hull to ride on top of the water.

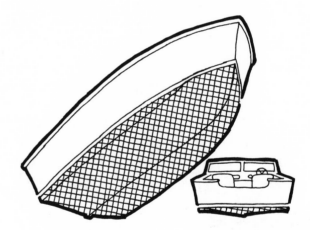

Tri-Hull: There are many shapes of tri-hulls, also called cathedral hulls. Basically, however, the tri-hull is three V-shaped hulls placed side by side. This provides an extremely stable platform. Speedy in smooth water, it is popular with fishermen, skindivers and waterskiers. The drawback to the tri-hull shape is that it pounds in rough water and can be quite wet from spray.

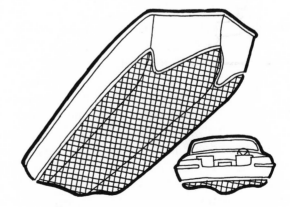

Boat Layout

Manufacturers sometimes use the same hull shape for several models, tailoring the interior arrangement of seating, storage and cabin areas for the varying needs of fishermen, waterskiers or cruising families. Some boat layouts are designed to serve several purposes well, so review your needs and expected boating plans before choosing a boat. Then choose a layout that serves your most important priorities.

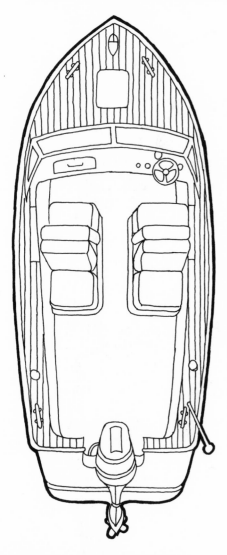 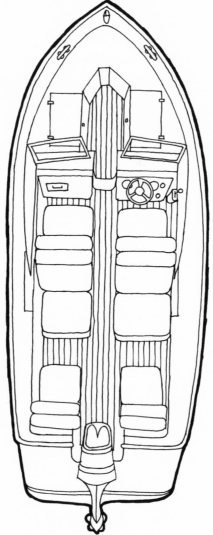 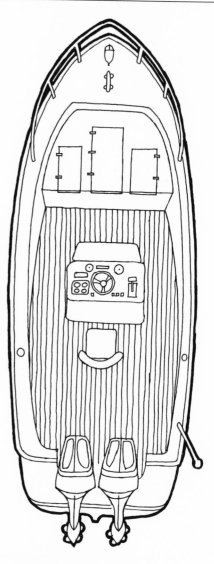

Runabouts: The most popular type of boat, the runabout is used for everything from water-skiing and fishing to daycruising. Protected by a windshield and featuring a covered deck forward, it usually has seats that can be folded flat into sunning pads. Folding tops with clear side panels add all-weather protection, but the runabout is primarily designed for speed and fun in the sun.

Bowrider: An offshoot of the runabout, but with an open area forward of the windshield with bench seating. Reached through a folding walk-through windshield, the area adds room during low-speed operation and provides more fishing space than a runabout, but it should not be used at higher speeds or in rough water. For spray protection, a snap-on tonneau cover is often supplied.

Center Console: This single-purpose boat is intended for the avid fisherman, although you'll find them used for waterskiing and day-cruising as well. With the steering console surrounded by walk-around cockpit, the fisherman can fight a fish without getting tangled up. This type of boat is also self-bailing, so the cockpit will drain away spray or rainwater. It usually comes with bait tanks and rod holders.

Overnighters and cabin cruisers differ from day boats primarily by having an enclosed cabin area (see cutaways below). Nevertheless, you can still pursue many day boat activities, such as waterskiing, fishing and diving on a cruiser. What you give up in cockpit room for cabin space you'll gain in the ability to spend whole weekends living on board, either at the dock or anchored, far from civilization.

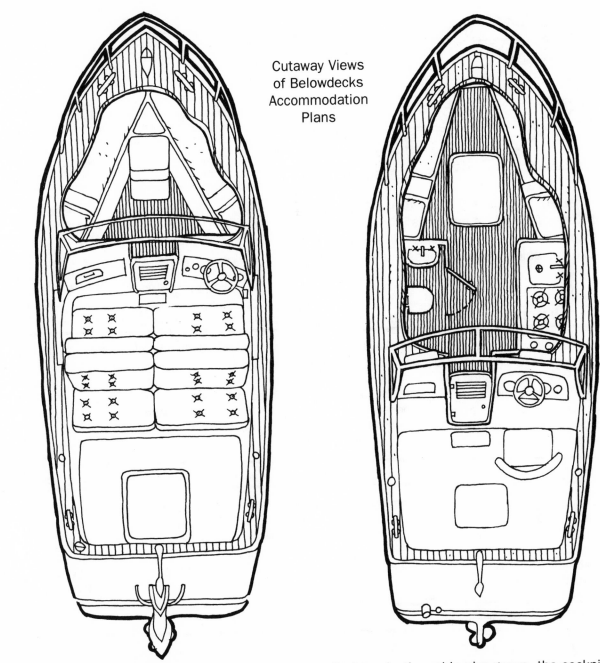

Cutaway Views of Belowdecks Accommodation Plans

Cuddy Cabin: Larger than a runabout but not quite a cruiser, the cuddy refers to the cabin area that often contains a pair of bunks with a portable toilet tucked between them. This allows a couple to overnight in reasonable comfort as well as providing added storage space for day cruising and the convenience of an onboard toilet.

Cruiser: As the cabin size grows, the cockpit room will diminish, but the emphasis of a cruiser is on living space belowdecks. In addition to permanent bunks, there may be a dinette that folds into a berth, the toilet may be in an enclosed compartment for privacy and the kitchen (galley) will have a sink with fresh water, an icebox and a stove.

Construction

Fiberglass is the most popular material for modern powerboats, providing flexibility, durability and low maintenance. Fiberglass construction is dictated by size and type of the boat as well as by the strength required of the hull. Less expensive fiberglass processes tend to produce less strength. Boat buyers should be aware of basic construction techniques. Variations are used in special-purpose boats.

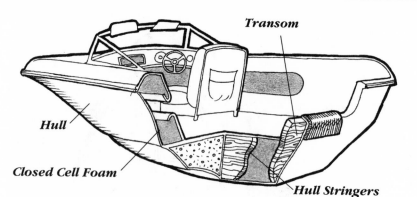

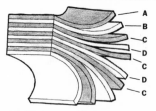

A hull is created by using resin reinforced with several different types of fiberglass materials in a sequence called a "laminate schedule." The resulting hull is watertight and rigid, as well as able to resist scrapes and damage.

A. The outer color layer is called gelcoat. It provides a smooth and glossy exterior finish that is also water-resistant.

B. Fiberglass cloth is often used to provide a smooth surface over thicker reinforcing fiberglass cloths.

C. Mat consists of random chopped fibers in a layer that absorbs resin and provides bulk.

D. Roving is a thickly woven fabric that provides strength against punctures and adds increased resilience to the laminate.

CONSTRUCTION METHODS: These will determine the strength and resilience of a hull and deck.

Chopper Gun is a machine that sprays random fibers and resin into a mold, or form, that gives the hull its shape. It is an inexpensive method best used on small power-boats where strength and impact resistance are not critical.	**Hand Layup** is the process of laminating a hull from fabric and resin by hand. Stronger than the chopper gun method, it is also more expensive and is common on high speed and offshore powerboats.	**Solid Fiberglass** is a hull built from layers of resin and fabric, without other reinforcing materials. It is the most common construction method in small powerboats.

REINFORCEMENT: Consists of a core sandwiched between layers of fiberglass for added strength and thickness.

Balsa Coring is done in a checkerboard pattern to prevent water seepage and is used to reinforce the hull or deck. Light and strong, it must be completely sealed in fiberglass to prevent rot.	**Foam Coring** is impervious to rot but is less resistant to impact and crushing from hard blows. Expensive, it adds insulation as well as strength.	**Plywood** is often used to reinforce decks, but must be protected from water leakage and rot. Cheaper than foam or balsa, plywood is also heavier.

SUPPORT: Where strength is required in specific areas, you may find the following materials.

Closed Cell Foam is used on many boats to provide flotation as well as to add strength and insulation against sound and moisture. In many cases, it fills all inaccessible areas of the boat.	**Hull Stringers**, beams that run fore and aft along the bottom of the hull, serve to support the cockpit floor and are used as engine mounts. These may be solid wood beams encased in fiberglass or fiberglass sections filled with foam.	**Transom** on outboard boats is usually extra-thick marine plywood sealed in fiberglass to support the engine. Sterndrive boats may have either wood or thick fiberglass transoms. Most inboards, which place little strain on the transom, use fiberglass.

Engine Choices

Modern powerboats have one of four engine arrangements: outboard, inboard, sterndrive or jet. Larger boats are sometimes equipped with a pair of engines. Two engines make maneuvering in tight quarters easier. Having two engines also provides "get-home" power in case one engine breaks down. The cost of operating and maintaining two engines will be higher than for a single one of equal horsepower.

Outboards: Less expensive than other engines, outboards provide the best power-to-weight ratio. They are available up to several hundred horsepower in V-8 configurations. With the engine mounted on the stern, outside the cockpit area, more interior area is gained for seating and moving around. Most outboards are two-cycle engines, requiring that oil be mixed with gasoline. The outboard tilts up to protect the propeller if it comes into contact with an underwater object. The engine can also be tilted to trim the boat for speed or balance.

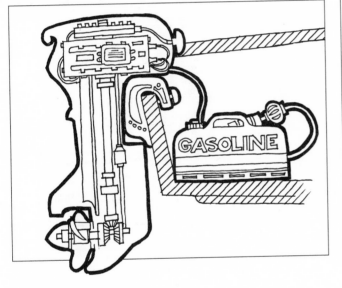

Sterndrive: Also called an inboard/outdrive, or I/O, the sterndrive combines an inboard engine with a drive system similar to an outboard's. Like the outboard, the drive will kick up in shallow water or when hitting an object. It can also be trimmed up or down to balance the boat. The engine is usually installed under a solid cover which takes up cockpit space, but the top is often covered with foam cushions and used as a sunning area. Powerful inboard engines can be installed that offer the convenient serviceability of an automotive-type motor.

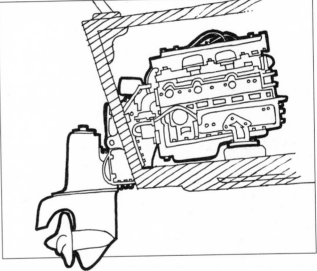

Jetdrive: This is most commonly found in waterski boats because it eliminates the propeller which can be dangerous to swimmers. An inboard engine is connected to a high-pressure jet pump that propels the boat with a stream of water, much like a firehose. Steering is accomplished by turning the direction of the jet nozzle. Reverse is achieved by redirecting the water backwards.

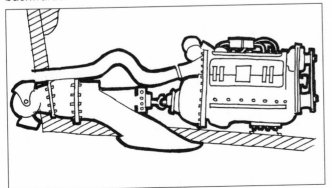

Inboard: These are rarely found on small trailerable powerboats, although they are an economical source of power. The propeller is exposed on the bottom of the boat, along with the prop shaft and rudder, making its use difficult in shallow water.

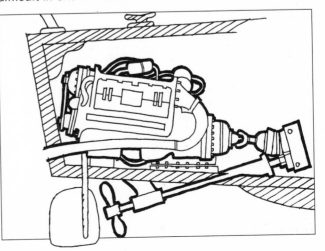

Comparison Shopping

Before you sign on the dotted line of a sales contract, shop around. Consider several different boats and check the prices at different dealerships. The comparison sheet below will help you compare boats, both for price and for equipment. It's often surprising how a boat that seems to be more expensive initially comes in at a lower price when you take into consideration the equipment that goes with it.

BOAT A

Brand _____

Type _____

Length _____

Power _____

Seating _____

People Capacity _____

Weight Capacity _____

Dealer _____

Delivery Date _____

Standard Equipment

_____

_____

_____

_____

_____

_____

_____

_____

_____

BOAT B

Brand _____

Type _____

Length _____

Power _____

Seating _____

People Capacity _____

Weight Capacity _____

Dealer _____

Delivery Date _____

Standard Equipment

_____

_____

_____

_____

_____

_____

_____

_____

_____

BOAT C

Brand _____

Type _____

Length _____

Power _____

Seating _____

People Capacity _____

Weight Capacity _____

Dealer _____

Delivery Date _____

Standard Equipment

_____

_____

_____

_____

_____

_____

_____

_____

_____

In considering your boat purchase, examine your own budget as well. How much down payment can you afford? What monthly payments will be comfortable? Do you have money set aside for maintenance, extra equipment and storage fees? How far will you trailer the boat? Is your present car capable of towing? How often? In deciding how much to spend, try to stay well below your maximum budget.

Optional Equipment

_____ $ _____
_____ $ _____
_____ $ _____
_____ $ _____
_____ $ _____
_____ $ _____
_____ $ _____
_____ $ _____

Total $ _____

Costs

Boat $ _____
Engine $ _____
Trailer $ _____
Options $ _____
Delivery Charge $ _____
Dealer Prep $ _____
Subtotal $ _____
Tax $ _____

Total Cost $ _____

Optional Equipment

_____ $ _____
_____ $ _____
_____ $ _____
_____ $ _____
_____ $ _____
_____ $ _____
_____ $ _____
_____ $ _____

Total $ _____

Costs

Boat $ _____
Engine $ _____
Trailer $ _____
Options $ _____
Delivery Charge $ _____
Dealer Prep $ _____
Subtotal $ _____
Tax $ _____

Total Cost $ _____

Optional Equipment

_____ $ _____
_____ $ _____
_____ $ _____
_____ $ _____
_____ $ _____
_____ $ _____
_____ $ _____
_____ $ _____

Total $ _____

Costs

Boat $ _____
Engine $ _____
Trailer $ _____
Options $ _____
Delivery Charge $ _____
Dealer Prep $ _____
Subtotal $ _____
Tax $ _____

Total Cost $ _____

Buying Tips

Like a car, a boat represents a major investment. In the long run, boats can be excellent buys, especially if they're well maintained; some may actually appreciate in value. So consider carefully before selecting a builder or a dealer, then use the following tips to get exactly the boat you want at the best price. A little homework and legwork can result in sizable savings. Buying at the end of the season can, too.

Finding the Right Boat
1. Comparison shop several builders at boat shows and get the names of dealers in your area.
2. Focus on major brands. Service and resale value are usually higher among more recognizable nationally manufactured boats than with small regional boat makers.
3. See what boats are popular in your area, and don't be shy about talking to other boatowners.
4. Read classified ads and check the selling price of similar-sized used boats. A sizable drop may indicate dissatisfaction or low buyer interest.

Finding the Right Dealer
1. Look for longevity in location, time-in-business and number of boat lines carried. New companies are more likely than old ones to disappear suddenly, but even old dealerships drop lines, leaving buyers without service facilities and parts.
2. Consider after-sale delivery service: Is there an on-site service department with personnel trained in both hull and engine repair? Are parts stocked?
3. Is the sales staff knowledgeable about the products? Do personnel have actual on-water experience with them?
4. Ask for a list of recent customers and contact them to find out about how they've been treated, before and after the sale.

Getting the Right Price
1. At boat shows, look for special offers, but be wary of those that include extra equipment you don't want.
2. Major builders may have several dealerships within easy driving distance. Shop around.
3. Compare price within a builder's line. Often the difference between the price of an 18- and a 20-foot boat is small enough to warrant choosing the larger boat.
4. Don't be afraid to dicker. A dealer may not lower the price on a popular model but he may throw in accessories on which he gets a discount.

To become better informed before inspecting a boat at a showroom or at a boat show, read a number of manufacturers' pamphlets and compare their construction claims. Make your own list of items to check or ask about. Take a knowledgeable friend (or two) along with you. Their informed opinions can provide a quick study of a complex task. Finally, take your time. Don't be rushed into a decision.

5. Boat prices are highest at the beginning of the summer season, lowest in the late fall. Shop at the right time.

6. Watch for introductory prices on new models. Builders sometimes underprice models in order to gain market acceptance.

7. Watch for discounts on discontinued models. Like the automobile industry, builders change colors and designs yearly, and dealers often discount older models to make room for delivery of new styles.

8. Demonstrators and boat show display models may command heavy discounts in exchange for a relatively small amount of wear and tear.

9. Buy from inventory, if possible, since dealers pay to have boats in stock and are more anxious to sell them than they are to order new ones for customers.

10. Don't load up on options. Order only those that have to be factory-installed. By shopping the discount marine hardware stores, you can save on accessories.

Choosing a Well-Constructed Boat

1. Inspect the nooks and crannies. If the builder takes care to do a good finishing job in areas you don't normally see, you can be assured he did the same in the rest of the boat. Sharp edges and loose strands of fiberglass are signs of hasty and sloppy construction.

2. Check the reflections along the side of the hull for "hard" edges, ripples and hollows. These represent distortions caused by inferior methods of attaching the bulkheads and interior parts to the hull interior. The smoother the hull, generally, the better the boat.

3. Look under important hardware, such as handrails and cleats to make sure that all fittings are through-bolted, not just screwed down, with backup plates of wood or metal underneath for stability and strength.

4. Examine hatches, dashboards and lockers for fit and construction. They should fit snuggly and be properly caulked.

5. Sturdy lengthwise beams, called stringers, support the engine and the flooring. If these are wood, they should be covered in fiberglass to protect the wood against rot. Better stringers are made of foam-filled fiberglass.

6. There should be a non-slip surface on the areas where you will be walking, such as the deck, the bow deck and along the sides.

7. Examine the electrical system carefully. Top-quality boats have color-coded wiring neatly bundled and accessible, circuit breakers rather than fuses and a factory-supplied wiring diagram for troubleshooting.

8. Most small powerboats have built-in fuel tanks. The best fuel tank material is fiberglass since it won't corrode. All tanks should be readily replaceable without dismantling the boat.

9. Examine the boat for design details. Quality boats have corners that are rounded for safety, handrails positioned for safe use and hatches sized for real humans. Try the seating and bunks for fit and comfort and make sure the visibility from the helm station is good in all directions.

Costs

Like buying a house or a car, purchasing a boat involves expenses above and beyond the cost of the boat itself. Being aware of what they are can influence how much you are willing to commit to the boat. From a practical standpoint, it is wise to put aside funds for future expenses. Down the road, there will always be an unexpected cost or some equipment or gear you will consider indispensable.

Registration: Nearly all states require that boats be licensed. Registration fees can range from a few dollars up to $50 and, like those paid for car registration, they are collected annually.

$ _____

Trailer License: Also an annual fee, the actual amount is usually a percentage of the trailer's value. The fee varies from state to state.

$ _____

Taxes: Many states assess personal property tax on boats. In others, taxes are levied by counties or cities. Check around to get an accurate idea of the amount involved.

$ _____

Loan Fees: The cost of boat loans, available from most financial institutions, varies considerably. Some institutions charge lower interest rates but more in processing fees. Others charge higher interest and lower fees. Comparison shopping can save money.

One-time fees (_____) Annual monthly payments (_____) Total $ _____

Insurance: This is a necessity. Shop around for the best price since premiums vary greatly among brokers. The speed and/or power of the boat, the number of engines, hull material, even your boating experience will be reflected in the annual rate. Brokers specializing in marine coverage often offer the best rates.

$ _____

Storage: Depending upon where you keep your boat, you can pay nothing (on a trailer in your driveway) to several hundred dollars a year (at a dock in an expensive marina). Since storage space is growing scarce as boating becomes increasingly popular, you can expect yearly increases for storage. If you keep your boat on the trailer, allow for launching fees.

$ _____

Maintenance: Set aside money for regular engine tune-ups and oil changes. All fiberglass boats should be waxed regularly to maintain the shine and, if you keep your boat in the water, you'll need to have the bottom painted with anti-fouling paint to prevent barnacles and other marine growth.

$ _____

Fuel: Marine engines tend to work harder than automobile engines because they are usually under full load, so fuel and oil consumption is greater. In addition, marine fuel docks charge more for gasoline than service stations. To save money, fuel up while on the trailer. Multiply the number of hours you anticipate using your boat during the year by the engine's hourly consumption at prevailing fuel prices in order to arrive at an annualized fuel figure.

$ _____

Depreciation: This is the good news for boatowners because in many cases boats depreciate relatively slowly compared to automobiles. There is an initial drop when you take the boat off the showroom floor but, after that, you may even find that your boat has either appreciated in value if you take good care of it or held its own in the market.

$ _____

Total First-Year Costs $ _____

Storage

How you plan to use your boat will dictate where and how you store it. If, for example, you plan to only cruise one specific body of water, you may wish to keep it there permanently. On the other hand, if you want to reach a variety of locations, you might opt to keep your boat on a trailer, the most inexpensive form of storage. Trailer storage also offers easy access for maintenance and improvement work.

Docking: A dock permits instant access to your boat, good protection and a place to work (usually with electricity and water), but the cost is highest.

Mooring: The boat is launched and ready for use but it is less protected and requires either launch service or your own dinghy to get to it.

Stacking: Popular in temperate climates, stack storage is inexpensive. The boat is not always ready for your use, however, and you can't sit or work aboard it while stacked.

Trailers/Tow cars

Trailering a powerboat gives you the freedom to explore new places, and it's surprisingly easy to do if you have the right equipment. The trailer you choose will depend on your boat's size and your plans. Your tow car should be powerful enough for the job (see the manual for towing capacities). Regular maintenance on the trailer will prevent on-road problems and keep your trailer in top condition.

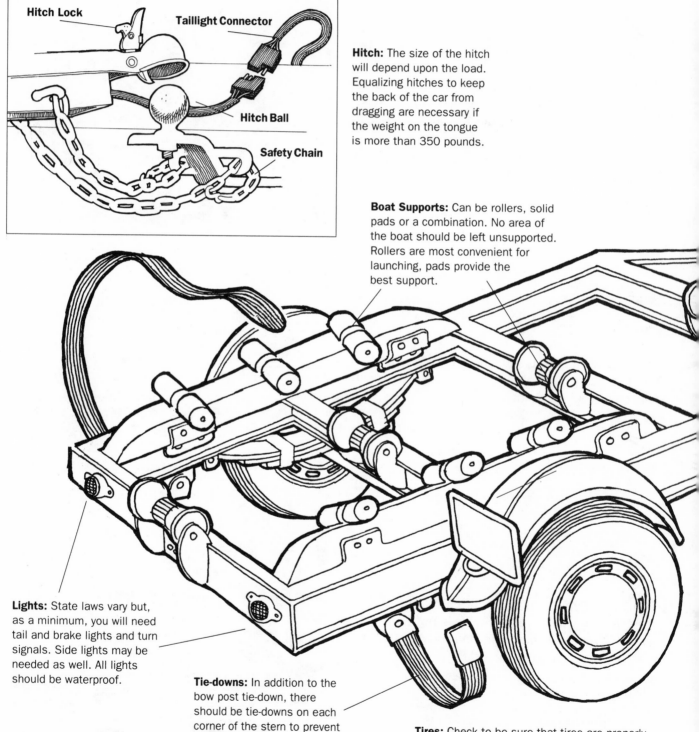

Hitch Lock

Taillight Connector

Hitch Ball

Safety Chain

Hitch: The size of the hitch will depend upon the load. Equalizing hitches to keep the back of the car from dragging are necessary if the weight on the tongue is more than 350 pounds.

Boat Supports: Can be rollers, solid pads or a combination. No area of the boat should be left unsupported. Rollers are most convenient for launching, pads provide the best support.

Lights: State laws vary but, as a minimum, you will need tail and brake lights and turn signals. Side lights may be needed as well. All lights should be waterproof.

Tie-downs: In addition to the bow post tie-down, there should be tie-downs on each corner of the stern to prevent sideways shifts.

Tires: Check to be sure that tires are properly inflated. A spare is essential unless the trailer uses the same tire size as the tow car.

Contrary to what your car dealer may say, you probably don't need a new car to handle towing a boat. In fact, many older cars have more powerful engines that are ideal for towing purposes. Investing in a tune-up or even a major overhaul may turn your older car into the perfect tow car. Consider improving the cooling and suspension systems because a small investment like this can make towing much easier.

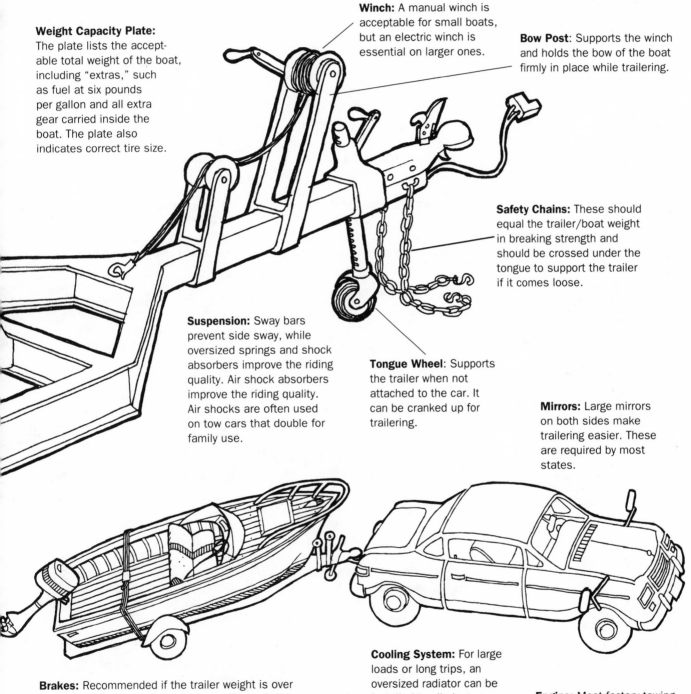

Weight Capacity Plate: The plate lists the acceptable total weight of the boat, including "extras," such as fuel at six pounds per gallon and all extra gear carried inside the boat. The plate also indicates correct tire size.

Winch: A manual winch is acceptable for small boats, but an electric winch is essential on larger ones.

Bow Post: Supports the winch and holds the bow of the boat firmly in place while trailering.

Safety Chains: These should equal the trailer/boat weight in breaking strength and should be crossed under the tongue to support the trailer if it comes loose.

Suspension: Sway bars prevent side sway, while oversized springs and shock absorbers improve the riding quality. Air shock absorbers improve the riding quality. Air shocks are often used on tow cars that double for family use.

Tongue Wheel: Supports the trailer when not attached to the car. It can be cranked up for trailering.

Mirrors: Large mirrors on both sides make trailering easier. These are required by most states.

Brakes: Recommended if the trailer weight is over 1,500 pounds. Brakes may be hydraulic or electric, controlled by cables to the tow car and activated when you press the brake pedal. Surge hydraulic brakes are simple and common since they are activated automatically when your car slows and the trailer "surges" forward.

Cooling System: For large loads or long trips, an oversized radiator can be installed to eliminate overheating. Oil coolers and transmission oil coolers, also aftermarket installations, can also add life to your engine while towing.

Engine: Most factory towing packages require the larger V-8 engines for power. Cars with automatic transmissions are fine, and 4–wheel drives can help at the launch ramp.

Coast Guard Equipment

Under the Federal Boat Safety Act of 1971, certain safety equipment is required aboard all boats. Boat-owners may request a courtesy boat examination by the Coast Guard Auxiliary which, if the boat meets the standards, will result in a Courtesy Motorboat Examination decal. These are minimum requirements. See pages 29 and 30 for additional recommended safety equipment and personal gear.

Class A (less than 16 feet)	Class 1 (16 feet but less than 26 feet)	Class 2 (26 feet but less than 40 feet)
One approved backfire flame arrestor on the carburetor of each gasoline engine.	One approved backfire flame arrestor on the carburetor of each gasoline engine.	One approved backfire flame arrestor on the carburetor of each gasoline engine.
At least two ventilator ducts fitted with airscoops for every engine and fuel tank compartment on gas-powered boats.	At least two ventilator ducts fitted with airscoops for every engine and fuel tank compart-ment on gas-powered boats.	At least two ventilator ducts fitted with airscoops for every engine and fuel tank compart-ment on gas-powered boats.
One Type I, II, III or IV personal flotation device for each person on board.	One Type I, II, III or IV personal flotation device for each person on board, plus one Type IV life cushion or ring buoy for throwing.	One Type I, II, III or IV personal flotation device for each person on board, plus one Type IV life cushion or ring buoy for throwing.
	One hand, mouth or power-operated horn or whistle audible for at least 1/2 mile.	One hand, mouth, or power-op-erated horn or whistle audible at least 1/2 mile.
		One ship's bell.
	One B-I approved portable fire extinguisher. Not required on open motorboats less than 26 feet where the design cannot trap gas fumes. Portable fire ex-tinguishers not required if a fire-fighting system is installed.	At least two B-I approved port-able fire extinguishers or one B-II portable extinguisher. If a fire-fighting system is installed in the engine compartment, one B-I portable extinguisher must also be aboard.
Navigation Lights: A white light visible 360° to a distance of at least two miles, and red and green bow lights visible for at least one mile.	Navigation Lights: A white light visible 360° to a distance of at least two miles, and red and green bow lights visible for at least one mile.	Navigation Lights: A white light visible 360° to a distance of at least two miles, and red and green bow lights visible for at least one mile.

See *Chapman Piloting* for equipment requirements for Class 3 information (vessels 41 feet to 65 feet).

In addition to carrying Coast Guard-required equipment, a boat must display state registration numbers on either side of the bow and have registration papers aboard. Specific state requirements vary. In most states, registration is handled by the motor vehicle department. The set of numbers you are issued identify your boat. They must be painted on or applied with decals in a color that contrasts with the hull's.

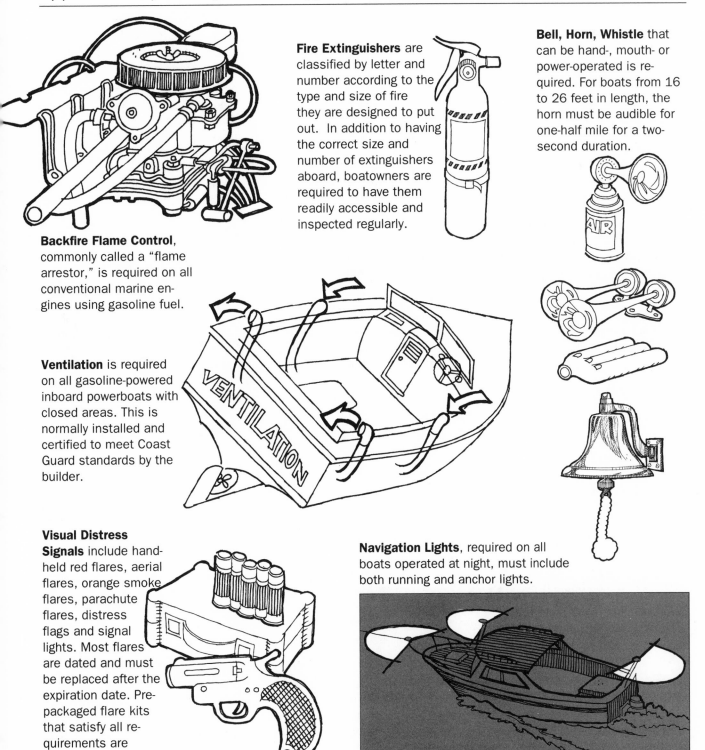

Backfire Flame Control, commonly called a "flame arrestor," is required on all conventional marine engines using gasoline fuel.

Fire Extinguishers are classified by letter and number according to the type and size of fire they are designed to put out. In addition to having the correct size and number of extinguishers aboard, boatowners are required to have them readily accessible and inspected regularly.

Bell, Horn, Whistle that can be hand-, mouth- or power-operated is required. For boats from 16 to 26 feet in length, the horn must be audible for one-half mile for a two-second duration.

Ventilation is required on all gasoline-powered inboard powerboats with closed areas. This is normally installed and certified to meet Coast Guard standards by the builder.

Visual Distress Signals include handheld red flares, aerial flares, orange smoke flares, parachute flares, distress flags and signal lights. Most flares are dated and must be replaced after the expiration date. Prepackaged flare kits that satisfy all requirements are available.

Navigation Lights, required on all boats operated at night, must include both running and anchor lights.

Coast Guard Equipment

You are required to have at least one Personal Flotation Device on board for each person on your boat. Aboard most small powerboats, your best choice is a PFD that members of your family feel comfortable wearing. The most popular model is the Type 3 "sports jacket" which can be worn continuously in comfort. It isn't as bulky as the Type 2 life vest and offers warmth and protection in cool, wet conditions.

Personal Flotation Devices (PFDs) are known to most people as life jackets. There must be one of the correct size and type-rating for every person on board. Each must be U.S. Coast Guard-approved and in good condition. Remember to keep them readily available for emergencies.

Type 1—Life Jacket
Bulky and traditional "Mae West" jacket, it is designed to turn an unconscious person face up. Accepted for all recreational and commercial boats. Used primarily on offshore commercial crafts.

Type 2—Life Vest
It can turn unconscious persons face up although it isn't guaranteed to do so. Acceptable on all recreational boats, it is recommended for both offshore and inshore use.

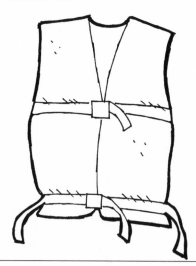

Type 3—Sports Jacket
Usually designed for waterskiing or sailing. Comfortable for continual wear, it is acceptable on all recreational boats. Intended for casual inshore use and sports.

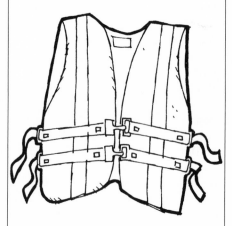

Type 4—Throwable
Designed to be thrown, acceptable as primary PFD only on Class A powerboats, canoes and kayaks. Acceptable only in conjunction with other PFD's on boats over 16 feet.

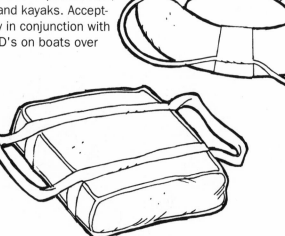

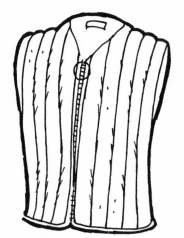

Extra Equipment

Federal laws and Coast Guard Auxiliary recommendations list the safety equipment you must or should have on board, but each boatowner will find other items that are essential to his or her sense of comfort, safety and enjoyment, as well as making the boat easier to handle and maintain. Some equipment should be ordered with a new boat, other gear can be added later.

Lines and Fenders: Dock lines are needed to tie up to a dock or mooring. Fenders protect your hull while tying up or moored to a pier.

Boathook: Useful for docking as well as picking up gear that has fallen overboard.

Flashlight and Spotlight: Should be waterproof and high-powered for on-board use. Also useful for identifying navigation aids at night.

Tool Kit: Stored in a rustproof case, the tool kit should include a selection of spare parts for the engine, such as spark plugs and fan belts, extra navigation light bulbs, wire and tape.

Boarding Ladder: Essential for swimming or skindiving, and a safety item for getting anyone back on board.

Binoculars: Helpful in picking out buoys or landmarks as well as for sightseeing. The 7x50 power is most appropriate for boating.

First Aid Kit: Should be in a waterproof container, with antiseptics, bandages and supplies for burns. Pre-packed first aid kits are often not sufficient. Consult your family physician for recommended supplemental supplies.

Compass: Useful even if you don't plan any long-distance navigation. Esssential on open water.

Navigation Equipment: The minimum is a chart of your boating area with a tide table where applicable. A parallel rule and pencil are essential in open water areas.

Electronics: A VHF radio, critical in an emergency, also provides weather forecasts and other information. A depth sounder is useful when navigating shallow waters. Other navigational electronics such as loran can be added as needed.

Canvas: For sun protection, have a Bimini or navy top installed at the factory or by your dealer. If you want protection from wind or spray, order a dodger or side curtains that have clear vinyl panels for visibility.

Anchor: Essential gear in any emergency that threatens to wash your boat up on shore, an anchor also comes in handy if you want to stop for a swim, picnic afloat or anchoring out overnight.

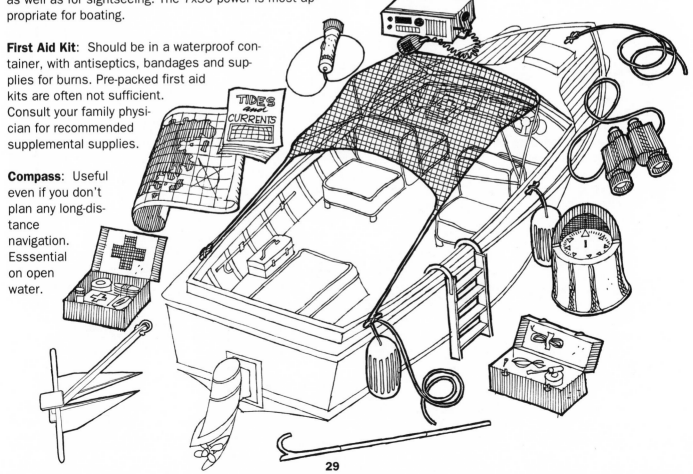

Personal Gear

In addition to having Coast Guard and recommended gear aboard, you'll want a selection of personal gear that can make boating more pleasant. When you're invited as a guest aboard a boat, it's always good manners to wear deck shoes, bring your own foul weather gear and carry your personal effects in a soft-sided duffel bag that is easy to stow. You'll also want to keep hat and suntan cream handy.

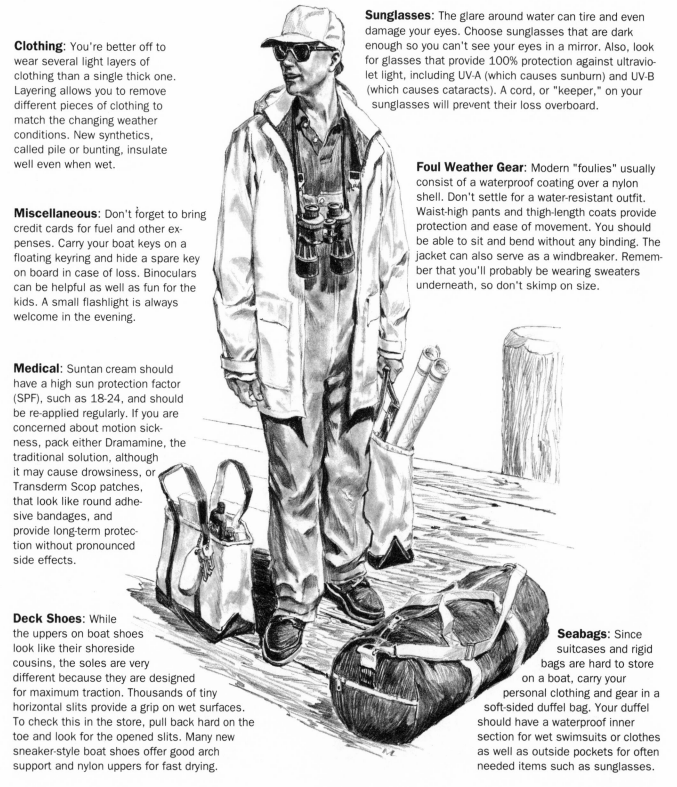

Clothing: You're better off to wear several light layers of clothing than a single thick one. Layering allows you to remove different pieces of clothing to match the changing weather conditions. New synthetics, called pile or bunting, insulate well even when wet.

Miscellaneous: Don't forget to bring credit cards for fuel and other expenses. Carry your boat keys on a floating keyring and hide a spare key on board in case of loss. Binoculars can be helpful as well as fun for the kids. A small flashlight is always welcome in the evening.

Medical: Suntan cream should have a high sun protection factor (SPF), such as 18-24, and should be re-applied regularly. If you are concerned about motion sickness, pack either Dramamine, the traditional solution, although it may cause drowsiness, or Transderm Scop patches, that look like round adhesive bandages, and provide long-term protection without pronounced side effects.

Deck Shoes: While the uppers on boat shoes look like their shoreside cousins, the soles are very different because they are designed for maximum traction. Thousands of tiny horizontal slits provide a grip on wet surfaces. To check this in the store, pull back hard on the toe and look for the opened slits. Many new sneaker-style boat shoes offer good arch support and nylon uppers for fast drying.

Sunglasses: The glare around water can tire and even damage your eyes. Choose sunglasses that are dark enough so you can't see your eyes in a mirror. Also, look for glasses that provide 100% protection against ultraviolet light, including UV-A (which causes sunburn) and UV-B (which causes cataracts). A cord, or "keeper," on your sunglasses will prevent their loss overboard.

Foul Weather Gear: Modern "foulies" usually consist of a waterproof coating over a nylon shell. Don't settle for a water-resistant outfit. Waist-high pants and thigh-length coats provide protection and ease of movement. You should be able to sit and bend without any binding. The jacket can also serve as a windbreaker. Remember that you'll probably be wearing sweaters underneath, so don't skimp on size.

Seabags: Since suitcases and rigid bags are hard to store on a boat, carry your personal clothing and gear in a soft-sided duffel bag. Your duffel should have a waterproof inner section for wet swimsuits or clothes as well as outside pockets for often needed items such as sunglasses.

Chapter 2

First Day Out

Pre-launch Checks

Just as aircraft pilots have extensive checklists for takeoffs and landings, powerboat owners will find a checklist can be a valuable reminder of equipment and procedures you don't want to forget. Your own pre-launch list should consist of some items to be checked off while still at home. You'll want to check off others moments before you launch your boat. Feel free to add to or amend the list, as necessary.

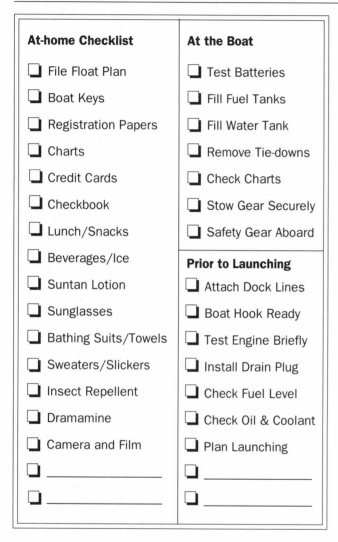

At-home Checklist

- ☐ File Float Plan
- ☐ Boat Keys
- ☐ Registration Papers
- ☐ Charts
- ☐ Credit Cards
- ☐ Checkbook
- ☐ Lunch/Snacks
- ☐ Beverages/Ice
- ☐ Suntan Lotion
- ☐ Sunglasses
- ☐ Bathing Suits/Towels
- ☐ Sweaters/Slickers
- ☐ Insect Repellent
- ☐ Dramamine
- ☐ Camera and Film
- ☐ _____
- ☐ _____

At the Boat

- ☐ Test Batteries
- ☐ Fill Fuel Tanks
- ☐ Fill Water Tank
- ☐ Remove Tie-downs
- ☐ Check Charts
- ☐ Stow Gear Securely
- ☐ Safety Gear Aboard

Prior to Launching

- ☐ Attach Dock Lines
- ☐ Boat Hook Ready
- ☐ Test Engine Briefly
- ☐ Install Drain Plug
- ☐ Check Fuel Level
- ☐ Check Oil & Coolant
- ☐ Plan Launching
- ☐ _____
- ☐ _____

At the Launch Ramp

You will want to load gear into the boat before launching and stow it out of the way so that you can move around easily. Heavy items, such as ice chests, should be placed as close to the center-line as possible to help balance the boat.

Attach bow and stern lines securely. You may want to have separate lines of extra length just for launching and retrieving your boat. Place the paddle and boathook for immediate use after launching.

Test the engine briefly to check battery by clicking the ignition switch momentarily. It's easier to remedy a dead battery while on the trailer than at the dock.

Install drain plug securely. Check the fuel level, the oil and the coolant.

Watch other boats being launched to see the methods used at this launching ramp. Check the water depth to make sure there is no sudden drop-off to cause trailer problems, and note any wind or current that may push the boat away after launching. Check to make sure steering, throttle and clutch controls are operating normally.

Check the drain plug again.

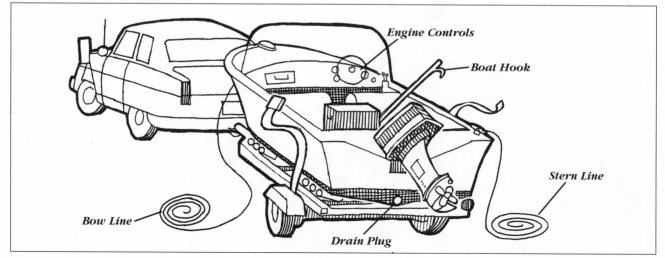

Engine Controls

Boat Hook

Stern Line

Bow Line

Drain Plug

A float plan is the boating version of an aviation flight plan. Before you go boating, leave a copy of the float plan with a responsible friend or relative (don't give it to the Coast Guard). If you have problems on the trip, this will make it easier for help to find you. When you return, be sure to inform the person to discard the float plan and, if you plan to stay longer, let them know so they won't start a search.

FLOAT PLAN

Today's date_____

Owner's name, address, phone number (and next of kin, if applicable):

_____

_____

Boat: Length_____ Make_____ Type_____ Color_____ Name_____

Radio: Type_____ Call sign_____ Raft/Dinghy_____

Engines: Type_____Horsepower_____ Number_____ Fuel capacity_____

Persons aboard:

_____
Name   Age   Address   Phone #

_____
Name   Age   Address   Phone #

_____
Name   Age   Address   Phone #

Departure: Date _____Time_____ Location_____

First destination: _____ Est. arrival date/time_____

          Est. departure date/time_____

Second destination: _____ Est. arrival date/time_____

          Est. departure date/time_____

Third destination: _____ Est. arrival date/time_____

          Est. departure date/time_____ Est. return/time_____

          In no event later than _____

If not returned by date/time_____, call the Coast Guard at _____

          or (local authority) at _____,

          and provide pertinent information.

Launching

Launching ramps can be busy places, particularly on summer weekends, so you and your crew want to be prepared to launch your boat smoothly and efficiently. Take a few moments to watch how other skippers are launching, since different ramps often require different techniques. Launching by sling is considerably easier on the boat, trailer and crew, but usually more expensive than launching at a ramp.

Before Backing Into the Water
Check to be sure that the winch cable is tight, and that the winch is locked. Remove the tie-downs.

If you have removable trailer lights, now is the time to disconnect them and store them in the car or trunk temporarily.

Outboards or sterndrives should have the drive unit raised to the "up" position so that it won't hit the bottom as you push the boat into the water. If there is a support bar under the drive unit for trailering, remove it.

Launching by Ramp
Align the trailer and car with the water and back up straight so that the trailer is at right angles to the water.

If possible, try to avoid submerging the trailer hubs unless they are waterproof. If you must put the hubs underwater, let them cool at least 15 minutes before launching. Hot bearings may be damaged by cold water.

When the trailer is in position, put the car's transmission in park, set the parking brake and place wooden chocks behind the two back wheels.

Release the winch and unhook the winch cable. Push the boat off the trailer while controlling it with the bow and stern lines.

Drive the car into the parking area and, if possible, hose off the trailer with fresh water to prevent rusting.

Move the boat promptly out of the launching area to allow others to use the ramp. Most ramps have docks or finger piers nearby.

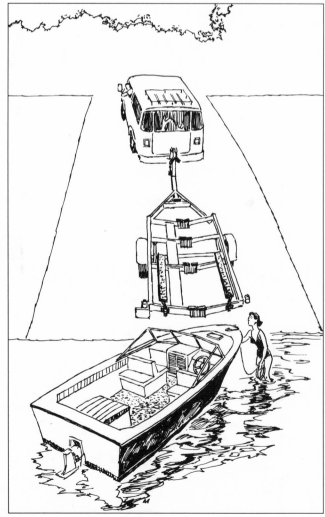

If there is a hose in the launch area, wet the bottom of your hull and carpeted trailer pads to make the boat slide off the trailer more easily. Be sure the hull drain plugs are in place and loose gear is stowed. After you've launched and taken the trailer to a parking place, take a moment to examine the trailer. Check for worn carpeting or rollers as well as rust spots that may be hidden when the boat is in place.

Launching by Sling

The sling operator will direct you where to park your car and trailer. You'll want to make sure that the slings provided by the operator are sturdy enough for your boat.

Placement of the slings is critical. Your boat dealer can tell you where they should go. If your boat has a raked bow, you may want to prevent the forward sling from slipping by tying the forward and aft slings together with a line.

As the boat is lifted off the trailer, control the swing with bow and stern lines. Under no circumstances do you want to walk under the hoisted boat or slings.

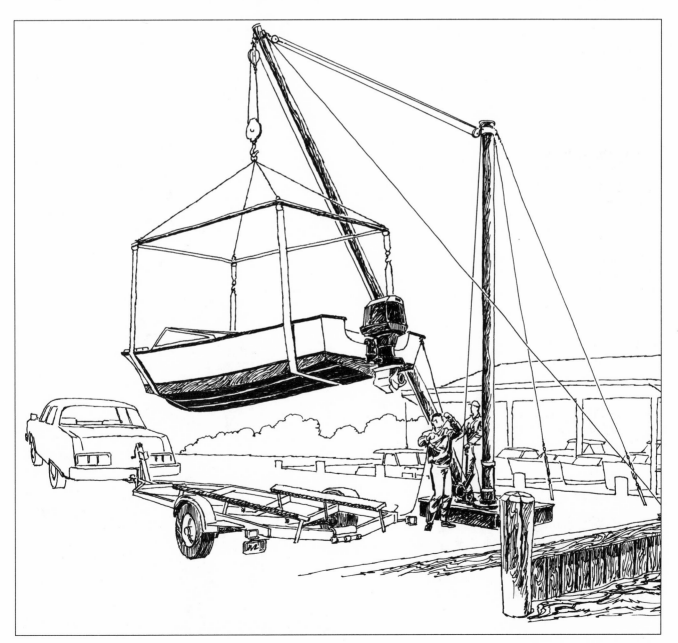

Tying Up to the Dock

The first real opportunity you'll have to practice your seamanship skills will come when you tie up to the dock. Just what method you use to tie up will depend upon many variables: the direction of the wind and current, other boats already at the pier and how long you plan to stay there. For short-term mooring (and for most purposes), however, a single bow line and a single stern line will suffice.

If possible, **dock your boat into the wind and current or on the downwind, or leeward, side of a pier** so that the wind pushes the boat away from the pier. This will reduce wear and tear on the hull and make your departure easier.

Before you tie up, **make sure that your bow and stern lines are ready for use.** If your dock line has a loop tied into the end, place the loop over the cleat on your boat and tie the other end of the line around the cleat on the pier. In this case, you will use the figure-8 cleating method. If there are no cleats on the pier, tie your dock lines to pilings on the pier using a clove hitch or a bowline knot (see pages 82-83).

It is a good idea to **attach the stern line to the side of the boat opposite the pier.** This provides a better angle and better leverage to hold the boat to the pier than attaching a stern line to the cleat nearest the pier.

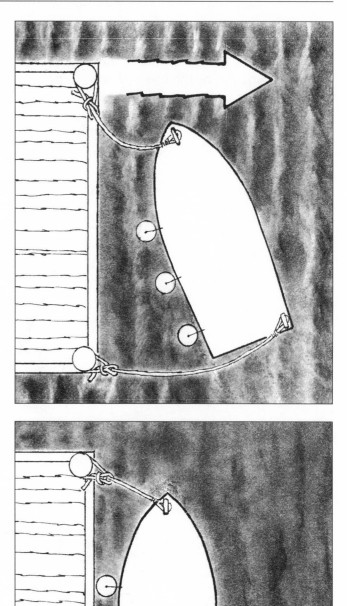

Fenders protect your hull from the pier and should be used even if the pier has protective padding since the padding may have nails in it. Two fenders are an acceptable minimum for most small powerboats, although three is recommended.

One fender should be placed at the widest point of the boat, the other located slightly forward of the stern. This allows the boat to lie alongside with good protection. If you have a third fender, place it forward for protection while approaching the pier.

Floating piers allow you to leave your boat for longer periods without worrying about the rise and fall of the tide. **If you leave your boat for several hours on a fixed pier, be sure to leave slack in your lines to allow for water level changes if there's a tide.**

Fueling the Boat and Starting the Engine

Fueling your boat is as simple as fueling your car although when fueling a boat there are some precautions you should observe. Most powerboats are extremely safe but gasoline fumes, being heavier than air, can gather in the bilge. A bilge blower, an exhaust fan designed to remove fumes from the engine compartment, is a useful device but there is no substitute for the human nose in detecting fumes.

On outboards with portable tanks, remove the tank from the boat and fill it on the gas dock. If you need to add oil, don't pour it in first. Add one gallon of gasoline, pour in the oil, then use the flow from the remainder of the gasoline to mix the oil.

Fueling

Turn off the engine, put out all cigarettes and shut down the electrical system. Keep a fire extinguisher handy and locate the nearest one on the pier. Close the companionway hatch.

If you wet the area around the gas filler on boats with built-in gas tanks, you'll be able to rinse off fuel spills easily afterwards. When filling a built-in tank, angle the fuel nozzle so that it makes metal-to-metal contact with the filler fitting to provide a ground thus decreasing chances of a spark.

After the tanks are filled, operate the blower, sniff the engine compartment and other closed areas for fumes, then start the engine.

Pre-start Procedures

Most outboard fuel tanks have air vents which must be opened, the fuel line connected securely to both tank and engine, and the priming bulb pumped until it feels firm. Make sure that the fuel tanks are not on top of the fuel lines or that sharp kinks in the line will not cut off the fuel supply.

Open up the engine compartment of a sterndrive or inboard and carefully sniff for gas fumes. Check the fuel pump and fuel filters for signs of leakage and let the blower run for at least five minutes before starting.

Starting Procedures

Sniff for fumes again, and then run the bilge blower for a few minutes. Many engines and outboards have cut-off switches to prevent the engine from starting except in neutral, so wiggle the shift lever to make sure that it is seated.

If the engine hasn't been run for some time, you may want to pump the throttle once or twice to squirt fuel into the cylinders. Too much can flood the engine.

If the engine has a choke, pull it out and turn the ignition key. If the engine doesn't catch immediately, depress the choke to keep from flooding the engine. If the engine doesn't start promptly, don't keep cranking until the battery is dead. Stop and investigate the problem (see page 110).

Steering

Steering, or helmsmanship, should seem natural to anyone who can drive a car. There are, however, very significant differences between a powerboat and an automobile. Inboard boats rely on a rudder to turn, while outboards and sterndrives turn away from the direction of the propeller thrust. In each case, the rear moves, rather than the front as in an automobile. This difference may take getting used to.

Whereas the front of the car changes direction when you turn the wheel, on the water **it is the stern of the boat that moves to point the bow in a new direction.** Actually the boat pivots with the stern moving more than the bow.

The most common mistake made by newcomers is to "oversteer" a powerboat, turning the wheel from side to side in an effort to keep the boat going straight.

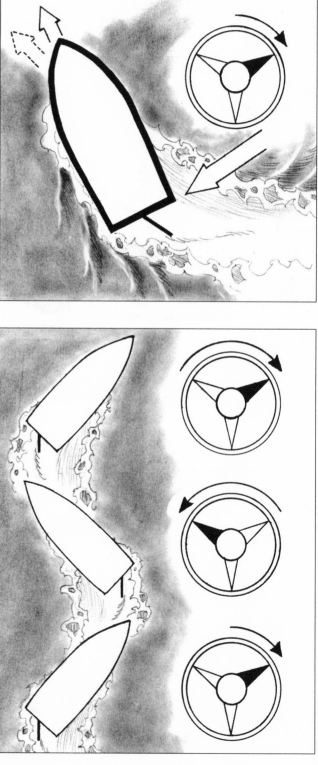

Just as with a car, **there is a "centered" position on the steering wheel** when the vessel will go straight. Because there's a time delay between turning the boat wheel and the boat's response, it's tempting to turn the wheel too far.

To overcome a zigzagging wake, avoid the large wheel movements shown at right. Instead, **move the wheel in small increments to maintain a steadier course.**

A boat requires less movement of the steering wheel than an automobile although it takes practice to learn just how far to turn the wheel on your boat to produce the desired result. Even while docking, you don't need to spin the wheel all the way in one direction or the other. Using a gentle combination of throttle and steering will accomplish more than frantically spinning the wheel from side to side.

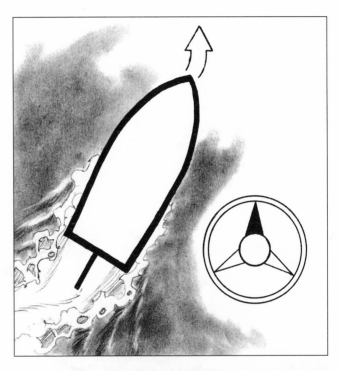

Experienced skippers learn to **return the wheel to the "centered" or neutral position** before the boat is actually lined up on the new course.

On boats that do not have an easily determined "top" or "bottom" to the wheel, a helpful way to know where the centered position is located is to place a piece of tape on the wheel at the top when the rudder, sterndrive or outboard is centered. On larger yachts, the tape is often replaced by a fancy knot called a "Turk's head."

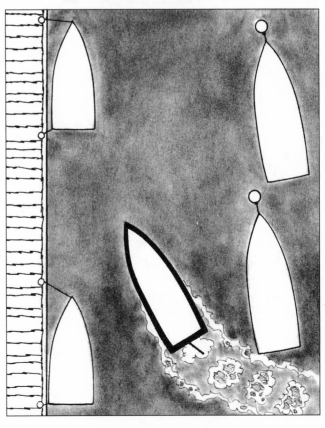

A powerboat can only be steered effectively while it is moving. Outboard or sterndrive boats are hard to steer when the propeller is not turning.

When maneuvering in close quarters, it is often hard to "coast." Under the circumstances, **steer by using small bursts of power** as well as occasional use of reverse if you need to brake.

Approaching the Dock

If you can park an automobile, you can dock a boat. You need to approach a dock slowly. Do not be afraid to back off and try again if things don't go as planned. Since the thrust of the propeller pushes the stern in the opposite direction to the direction you turn the steering wheel, steering a boat is more a case of steering with your stern. In close quarters, try to keep an eye on your stern's location.

Make your approach at an angle of about 30° to the dock. As your bow nears the dock, turn the wheel away from it. This will swing the stern inwards to help line the boat up parallel to the dock. Dock lines should be securely attached to bow and stern cleats in advance.

Move the shift lever into neutral, and start turning the steering wheel back toward the dock as the boat slows down. You may want to hand the bow line to someone on the dock or have a crew member step ashore with it.

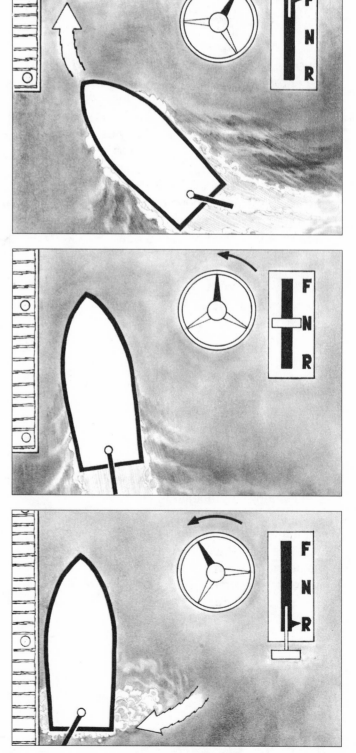

With the steering wheel turned toward the dock, shift into reverse for a moment. This will stop the boat's forward motion and pull the stern toward the dock. **The remaining dock lines can then be secured on shore.**

Leaving the Dock

Departing a dock is essentially the reverse of arriving. Skippers sometimes forget that turning the steering wheel away from the dock does not turn the bow away. It pushes the stern inwards against it, and it is not uncommon to see a boat bumping along a pier trying to turn outwards without success. To prevent this from happening, angle the bow away from the pier before trying to turn away from it.

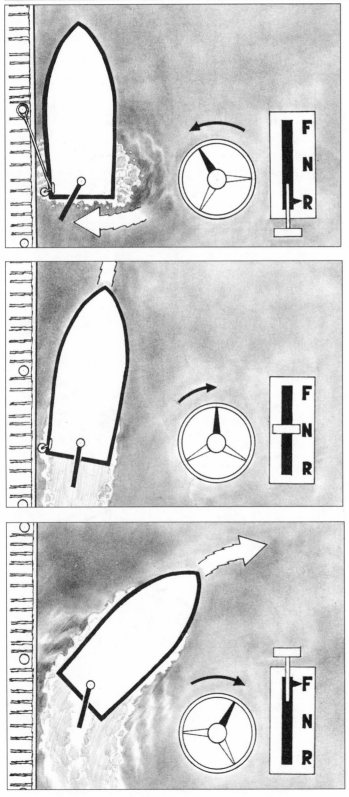

On a small boat, one of your crew can:
Push the bow away from the dock to give you the necessary room to start turning.

On a larger boat, or when wind or current is pushing your boat against the pier:
Put a fender between the stern of your boat and the pier and untie all the dock lines except for one, a spring line cleated amid ships on the dock and leading to the stern.

Turn the wheel toward the dock, and put the shift lever into reverse. This will start the bow moving away from the dock.

When your bow is away from the pier:
Center the steering wheel, put the engine in neutral, and untie your stern line from the dock. This should all be done quickly, particularly if the wind or current is pushing you back against the dock.

With the stern line aboard put the shift lever in forward and steer away from the dock. Make sure that you don't turn sharply until you are away from the pier or your stern may swing into the dock. As you maneuver away, check for traffic around you.

You're now on your way!

Rules of the Road

The Rules of the Road were devised to prevent collisions. They provide for right of way in different situations. The International Rules of the Road govern offshore encounters. However, the Inland Rules of the Road cover the right of way on lakes, rivers and even coastal harbors. The most common rules are illustrated and described on these pages. For a complete listing, see *Chapman Piloting*.

Definitions

Vessel: Every type of watercraft capable of being used as a means of transportation on the water.

Motorboat: Any vessel propelled by machinery, including sailing vessels under both sail and power.

Sailing Vessel: Any vessel which is under sail alone.

Right of Way: The right (and duty) to maintain course and speed.

Privileged Vessel: The vessel which has the right of way. A privileged vessel is expected to maintain its course and speed.

Burdened Vessel: The vessel which must keep out of the way of the privileged vessel.

Safe Speed: A speed that takes into consideration visibility, traffic on the water, moored or anchored boats, obstructions in the area and maneuverability of the vessel.

Meeting Situations

When two motorboats meet head-on or nearly so, each vessel should turn to starboard, so that it will pass the other port to port. In this case, neither vessel is privileged. Both must make efforts to pass correctly.

If, for convenience or safety, a starboard-to-starboard passing is desired, either vessel may signal its intention with two short horn blasts. The other should answer with two short blasts of its own.

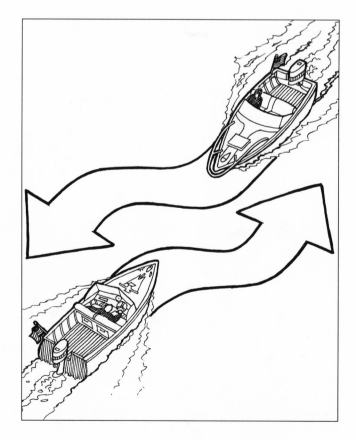

While the Rules of the Road cover many possibilities, the most common on the waterways is the crossing situation. If you are the privileged vessel and plan to change your course, make that change early so that you don't confuse the burdened vessel at the last moment. Remember, too, that by changing course you may lose your privileged vessel status. It is often better to change course *after* crossing.

Danger Zone: The area from directly ahead to 112.5° on the starboard side.

Crossing Situations

A crossing situation, as the term implies, involves two vessels approaching each other at an angle where one will cross the other's path. The rule governing this situation is straightforward. At some point, one vessel will be in the other's danger zone. When that occurs, the vessel that has the other in its danger zone must either slow down or stop and let the other pass by. Thus, skippers are most watchful for traffic forward and to starboard, knowing that any vessel appearing in that sector has the right of way. On many rivers, however, there is an exception to this rule. Vessels crossing the river must keep clear of vessels traveling up or down it. The privileged vessel in each instance is expected to continue on the same course and at the same speed.

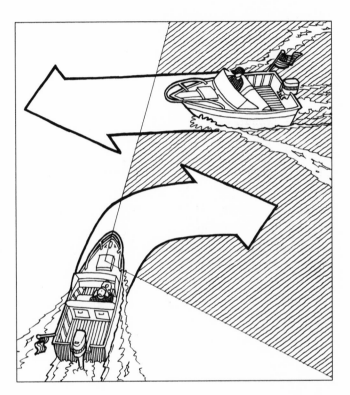

Overtaking Situations

When two motorboats are moving in the same direction and the vessel astern desires to pass, it must keep clear of the vessel ahead. When passing another vessel on its starboard side (as shown at right) the horn signal is one short blast. The signal for passing the other vessel on its port side is two short blasts. If the course ahead is safe for passing, the right-of-way vessel answers with the same number of short blasts. If the course is not safe, the privileged vessel either fails to answer or answers with five or more short blasts to indicate danger.

Rules of the Road

As a rule, sailboats have right of way over power. Nevertheless, sailboats may have their sails hoisted while also using their auxiliary engine, making it hard to determine whether they have right of way or not since their status depends on how they are powered. If there is any question, assume that the sailboat has the right of way and keep your distance since it may change course unexpectedly.

Boats Powered by Sail

A boat propelled by sail, oars or paddles has the right of way over motorboats because it is considered to be less maneuverable. The only exception occurs when a sailboat or other non-powered vessel actually overtakes a motorboat and intends to pass it. At that point, the sailboat loses its privileged status and must give right of way to the powerboat.

Narrow Channels

A motorboat nearing a bend in a channel where approaching vessels cannot be seen will signal with one long blast (4-6 seconds), which should be answered by any approaching motorboat within hearing distance. Motorboats should keep to the starboard side of narrow channels whenever it is safe and practical.

While the Rules of the Road clearly define "right of way" and "burdened" vessels, the underlying intent is to prevent accidents. Even though you may have the right of way in a given situation you are still expected to avoid collisions and may be held liable if you do not take preventive action when you see a dangerous situation developing. There's no substitute for prudence and common sense on the water.

Fishing Vessels
A fishing vessel using nets, lines or trawls has the right of way over motorboats and sailboats, but it must not obstruct channels used by other boats.

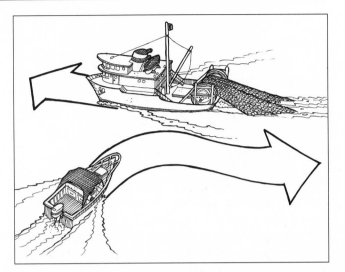

Leaving Docks
A vessel moving in a channel normally has the right of way over vessels leaving a dock. There is one exception: Ferryboats are given right of way leaving the dock. Other vessels must keep clear.

Ships
While ships are governed by the same right-of-way rules as powerboats, they lack the ability to maneuver or stop as quickly, so smaller boats should stay clear. When a ship is in a narrow channel and unable to change course, it becomes the privileged vessel.

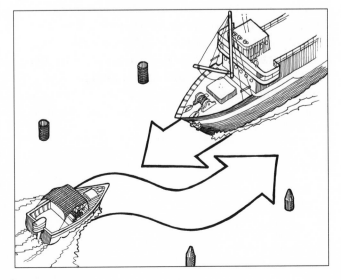

Common Hazards

On large ships, lookouts keep an eye out for waterborne traffic and other potential hazards. On a small powerboat, the task falls to the skipper who, by controlling the vessel's wheel and the engine throttle, commands in what direction and at what speed the boat will go. The skipper's main concern will be with the body of water lying ahead of the boat and to the right, the right-of-way danger zone.

Spotting Wakes

The most common hazard on the water is the wake of another boat or ship. Large ships push aside a huge amount of water resulting in large wakes. Even motoryachts can create sizable wakes. Hitting such a wake at high speed is a frequent cause of accidents.

The wake from a large vessel trails out from its bow and stern at 45° angles. Even at a distance, wakes can make bumpy riding for smaller boats in the vicinity. The best strategy in the company of sizable vessels moving through the water fast is to throttle back, noting the direction and size of their wakes.

Handling Wakes

The first thing to do when you spot a large wake is to slow down and check the direction it is moving in. Heading directly into a wake can cause your boat to drop into the trough between waves and nose into the next wave. You do not want to take a wake directly on the stern or amidships. The best way to cross is at a slight angle, so that your boat eases up each wave, then slides down into the trough without pounding.

Lobster pot buoys, or markers, and fishing nets, or stakes, are often found grouped in areas where the fishing is good. If you see a marker, keep your eyes open for others. Sometimes markers appear set at random, but in many areas they extend in a "line" that is predictable. Don't motor too close to the markers or stakes because loose line floating just below the surface nearby can foul your propeller.

Fishing Nets and Lobster Pots

These are often found on the water within site of the shore and can usually be spotted by the colored buoys that support them. Sometimes, in the sparkle of the afternoon sun or at high tide when they may be partially submerged, it takes concentration to locate them. Crab and lobster pots usually have a nylon line that may wrap around your propeller and stall the engine. The best policy is to give all such markers and floats a wide berth.

Clearing a Fouled Propeller

If you do run over a marker and foul your propeller with the line, your engine will strain against the load and die. With an outboard or sterndrive, you can clear away tangled line by raising the drive unit out of the water and cutting the rope with a sharp knife. Be sure that you get all the pieces, including those that may have pulled into the space between the propeller and the drive unit. This will prevent burnt bearing problems at a later date.

If you have an inboard, or cannot raise the drive unit, you can tape or lash the knife to the end of your boathook. By leaning over the side, you can cut away most of the tangle. If the water is calm, you can dive overboard with the knife, but this should not be attempted if the boat is bouncing around in waves.

Common Hazards

Logs and driftwood are year-round problems in some areas, such as the Pacific Northwest, and a seasonal hazard elsewhere. You can expect to see more semi-submerged objects after a rainstorm, for example, when logs and driftwood are carried into boating areas by rivers that have risen above their normal level. Try to stay away from river outlets after a storm and slow your boat down when passing through debris.

Logs and Driftwood

In many parts of the country, particularly those areas with forested shorelines, skippers should keep a sharp lookout for floating wood. Other areas, such as harbors and ports, may have debris in the water. Hitting a floating object in a small powerboat usually does no hull damage but it can bend or break a propeller blade. Watch the water ahead for any unusual spots that don't have the same motion as the surrounding water. A semi-floating log or piece of debris lying just below the surface will affect the action of the waves. In these areas, many powerboat skippers find it wise to carry a spare propeller and the tools needed to change a damaged prop. Remember: The slower the speed the less the potential for damage.

Visual clues often suggest the presence of obstructions or hazards below the water's surface. A beach that slopes gradually is likely to continue at the same angle underwater, for example, making for shallow water. If there is a derelict warehouse along the shore, the remains of a pier are likely to be in the water nearby. Boulders piled along the shore are a good indication that there will be underwater rocks as well.

Shallow Water/Underwater Obstructions

Every boating area has shallows. Until you've become familiar with charts and buoys that show you where these areas are located, proceed with caution. Underwater obstructions may include old pilings that have broken off below the surface, rocks or even sunken vessels. One way to avoid these, in the absence of a chart, is to watch where other boats go as well as areas they avoid. Don't be shy about asking other skippers for tips on shallows or obstructions. They may have found them the hard way—and save you the expense and embarassment of finding them yourself.

Anchor Lines

You'll find anchored boats in every boating area. Anchor lines, or rodes, pose a potential hazard because they may lie underwater at a shallow angle, invisible to the passerby. Since they may extend far out in front of a boat, be sure to leave plenty of clearance when passing the bow of an anchored vessel.

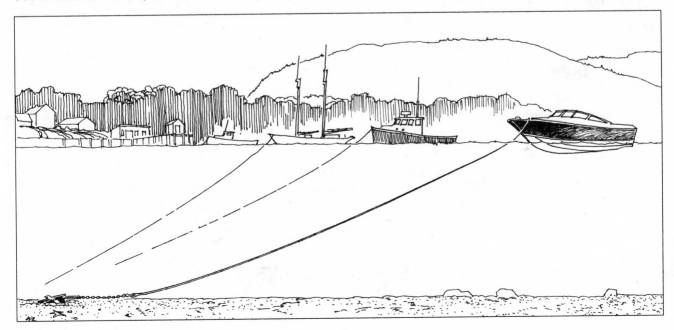

Charts and Maps

Charts are to skippers what road maps are to drivers—essential whether one is venturing into new areas or revisiting familiar places. A chart shows how to get from one point to another and alerts you to hazards along the way. It also shows the location of waterborne aids and landmarks on shore to help you find your position. Chart reading, a basic boating skill, is as straightforward as reading a highway map.

Types of Charts

Charts for your area are available at your local marine store. Just as you can get a map of an entire state or just one city, nautical charts may show an entire coastline or a single harbor in great detail. The Small-Craft Charts come in handy booklet form for easy storage. They contain the most important parts of larger charts and often offer such additional information as lists of local marinas or services.

Basic Chart-reading

Water depth on most coastal and inland charts is indicated in feet. Contour lines show underwater ledges, ridges and drop-offs. Colors are used to indicate different depths: yellow is commonly used for land; light blue for shallow water; white for deeper waters.

Chart Symbols

Navigational aids, salient features on land and underwater hazards are indicated with a variety of symbols. Some common ones are shown below:

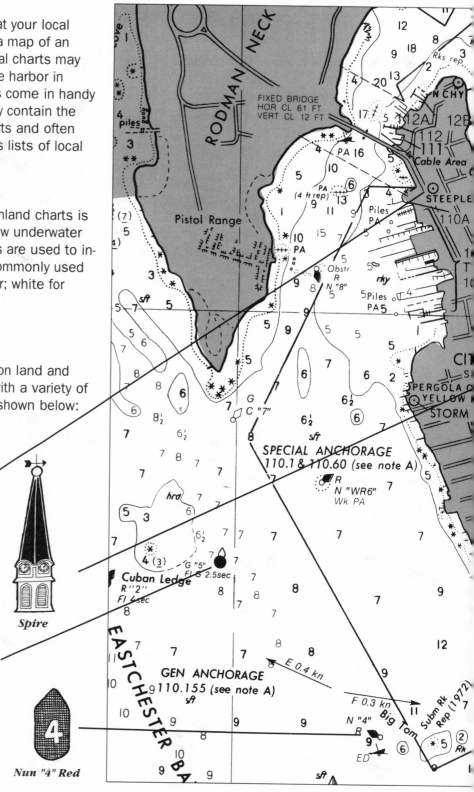

Steeple

Spire

Gong "5"

Nun "4" Red

Landmarks along the shore are represented on charts by easily recognized symbols, as is important information about what lies beneath the surface. The landmarks are useful as checkpoints en route to a destination. Anticipating and avoiding underwater hazards by recognizing their presence and position on a chart can be even more important in both planning a trip and exploring new waters.

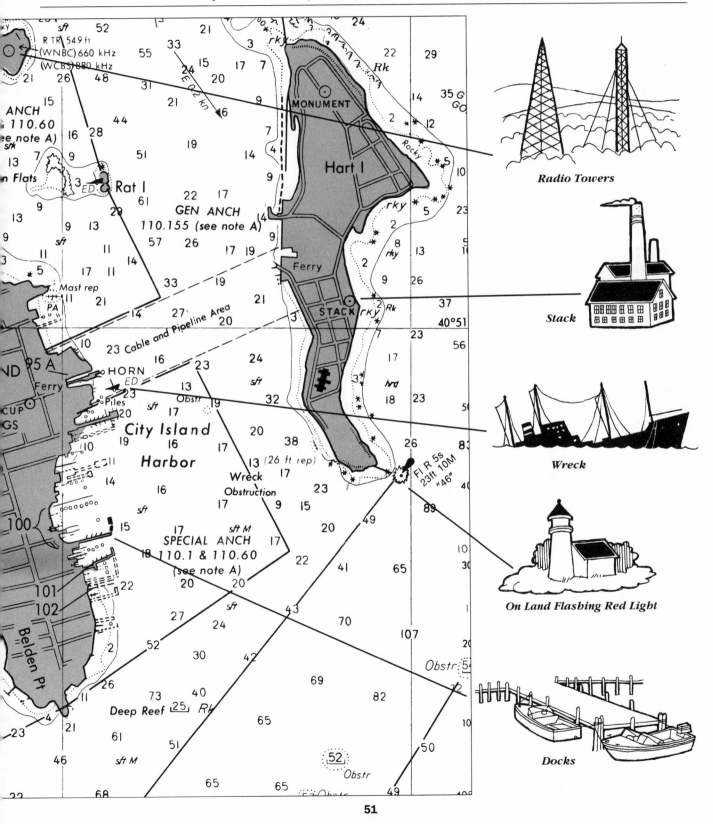

Radio Towers

Stack

Wreck

On Land Flashing Red Light

Docks

Buoys

Color- and number-coded buoys mark channels and warn of danger. Conical nun buoys are painted red, even numbered and generally kept to the right when entering a river or returning to a harbor. Cylindrical can buoys are black or green, odd numbered and kept to the left when returning. Day beacons are fixed rather than floating marks used in shallow water. See *Chapman Piloting* for a complete listing.

Navigable Waters: The buoy system used along both coasts and on the Great Lakes. The rule of "Red, Right, Returning" applies when entering a harbor from seaward.

The Intracoastal Waterway: This system runs parallel to the Atlantic and Gulf Coasts from New Jersey to the Mexican border. Aids have some portion marked with yellow but otherwise follow the Navigable Waters system, with red on the right clockwise around the U.S.

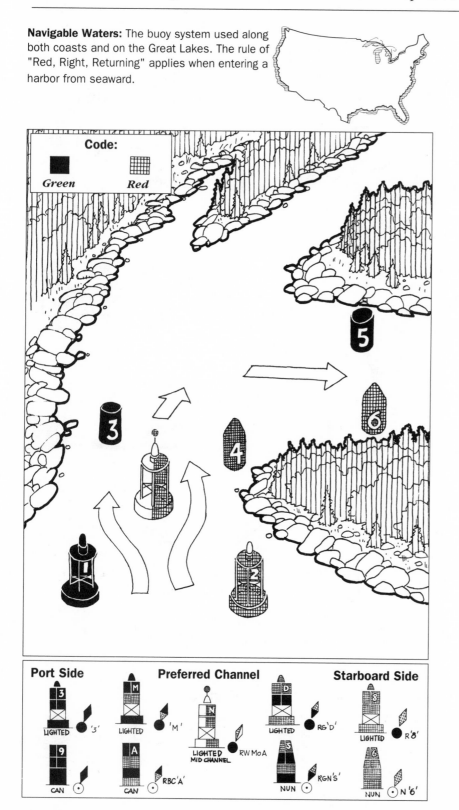

Code:

Green   Red

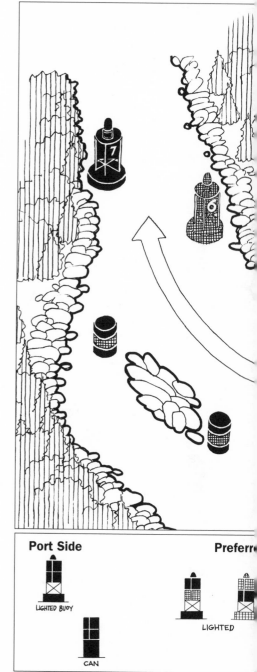

Port Side   **Preferred Channel**   **Starboard Side**

3 LIGHTED '3'	M LIGHTED 'M'	N LIGHTED MID CHANNEL RW MoA	D LIGHTED RG'D'
9 CAN	A CAN RBC'A'	S NUN RGN'S'	6 NUN N'6'

3 LIGHTED   R'8'

Port Side   **Preferr**

LIGHTED BUOY   CAN

LIGHTED

Special purpose buoys include: vertically striped buoys that indicate the middle of the channel; lighted buoys, either green with green lights or red with red lights; bell buoys and gongs, activated by waves; and horns or whistle buoys that are battery-powered. If, in fog, you suspect you are near a bell buoy or gong but the water is calm, you can activate it with your boat's wake by turning in tight circles.

Western Rivers: Red buoys are on the right when moving upstream. The numbers on lighted buoys reflect the mileage from some reference point.

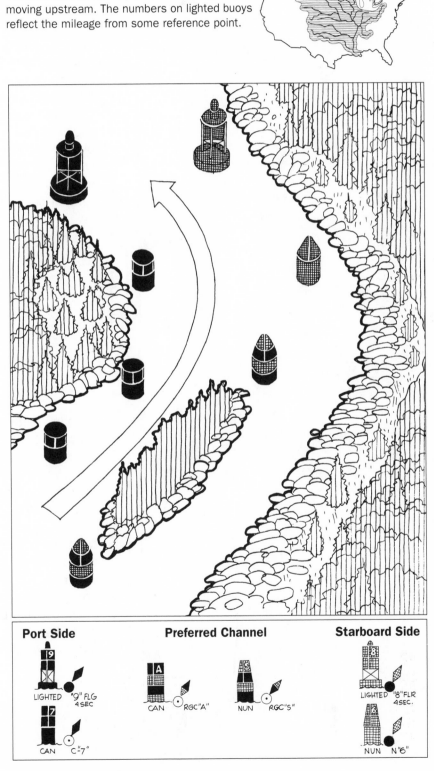

Port Side   Preferred Channel   Starboard Side

LIGHTED "9" FLG 4 SEC

CAN "A" RGC "A"

NUN RGC "5"

LIGHTED "8" FLR 4 SEC.

CAN C "7"

NUN N "6"

Docking in Wind and Current

Wind or current may sometimes push you toward or away from the pier where you intend to dock. To find the direction and force of the wind or current, stop your boat someplace nearby and see which way it drifts—and how fast. Armed with that knowledge, you can plan your docking approach and avoid surprises. When wind and current come from opposite directions, they sometimes cancel each other out.

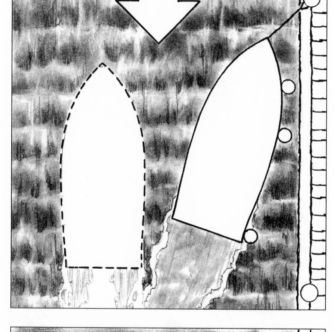

Docking With Wind or Current Parallel to Pier
Whenever possible, head into the wind or current. It will help slow your boat down. Match your speed to nature's forces so your boat stops at the place you want to tie up. Angle the boat in toward the pier gently, being careful not to let the current or wind push you in too fast. As soon as the bow is close to the dock, attach the bow line and let the wind or current push the stern in against the pier.

Docking With Wind or Current Toward Pier
Stop the boat parallel to the position you want on the pier and let the wind or current push you sideways into place. Remember, however, to use fenders because the boat will be continually forced against the pier by the elements.

Docking With Wind Away From Dock (not shown)
With the wind pushing you away from the dock, you must use the throttle and shift to keep the boat near the dock. Secure the bow line to the dock first and then turn the wheel toward the dock. By using reverse, you can pull the stern into the dock easily to secure the stern line.

Tying Up Overnight

With the boat tied up at a pier or slip, the crew can leave the vessel overnight or sleep aboard it without worry. When tying up, it's best not to create a spider web of lines. Instead, use a few critical dock lines that protect the boat against shifts of wind or current, or even the occasional midnight squall. The use of fenders is a must in most situations. Also keep in mind a rise and fall in the water level if relevant.

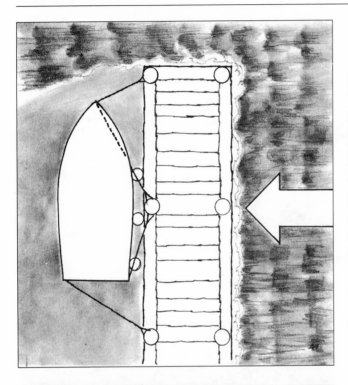

Overnighting at a Pier

Try to choose the side of the pier that will offer the greatest protection from wind and current, and ask other skippers what effect a shift during the night has on boats. Four dock lines are enough for most small powerboats: a bow line, a stern line (from the outside corner), two spring lines: one from the inside stern to a cleat on the pier near the middle of the boat; the other from the bow cleat to the same cleat near the middle of the boat. The spring lines serve to keep the boat from moving forward or backward, as well as holding the flat side of the hull where the fenders can protect it. It is also correct to run spring lines from a middle cleat on the boat forward and aft to the dock.

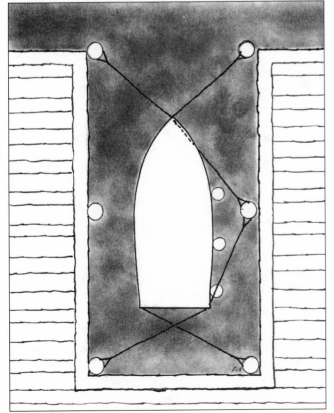

Overnighting in a Slip

A bow and stern line to each side of the slip will hold the boat away from the piers. Spring lines, docking lines that run at an acute angle from the dock to the boat, help keep the boat from moving back and forth if you plan to stay aboard.

Hauling Out/Retrieving by Sling

Retrieving your boat from the water essentially reverses the steps you took to launch it. At the end of a long boating day, it's a great temptation to rush through the procedure. Take the time to make sure that your boat is properly seated on the trailer, both for correct support and for balanced trailering. Also, pull the drain plugs at this time to drain any water from the bilge.

At the Pier
With an outboard, disconnect the fuel line and let the engine idle until it runs out of fuel. This prevents the formation of deposits in the engine.

Outboards and sterndrives should be tilted to the up position to simplify loading the boat onto the trailer.

Retrieving the Boat at the Ramp
Before backing the trailer, hook the winch cable to the back of the trailer so it can be reached easily from the boat and hauled to the bow eye.

Back the trailer squarely into the water so that the boat is aligned on the rollers and pads. If the trailer is angled, the boat will not rest on it properly. Chock the car's tires and put the transmission in park.

Hook the winch cable to the bow eye and guide

the bow of the boat to the first roller or trailer pad. (When using an electric winch and wire cable, wear gloves for protection and operate the winch by remote control. Do not stand near it, since a broken cable can whiplash dangerously.)

Keep the boat centered and aligned, and don't be embarrassed to start over if it isn't lined up correctly. Once the boat is completely on the trailer, put the car in low gear and pull the trailer slowly up the ramp.

Re-install the stern tie-down straps or lines, fit the sterndrive support bar in place and hook-up the trailer lights.

Before leaving the ramp area, check the boat to make sure that nothing can blow out, that the canvas top is secured, and that all loose objects are stowed away.

Regardless of the method you use to haul out, don't rush away from the ramp or hoist area until you are sure that everything is ready for trailering. You can usually move the boat at low speed without tying it down, but the bow and stern tie-down straps should be in place before you reach the highway. Also check the trailer lights and secure all loose items inside the boat or stow them in the car trunk.

Retrieving the Boat by Sling

Since wet boats are slippery, you may want to tie the slings together for security before lifting the boat out of the water. While positioning the slings, keep your hands away from the boat so they won't be caught when the slings tighten.

Use the bow and stern lines to position the boat properly over the trailer. Under no circumstances should you walk under the boat.

If the boat doesn't settle properly on the trailer, ask the sling operator to lift the boat slightly and re-position it. Don't attempt to move the boat on the trailer without lifting it beforehand.

Trailering

Safe and easy trailering depends on preparation and practice. Once you know the basics, towing a trailer is simple. Backing it up is more difficult. Remember that no one is a "natural" at backing a trailer, and even the experts needed time to master the tricks. Before you drive off to launch your boat at a busy ramp, take time to practice backing the trailer in a deserted parking lot or empty field.

Pre-trailering Checklist

- ☐ Remove or stow loose items that might blow out of the boat.

- ☐ Make sure that objects such as anchors and batteries are secure and don't slide around.

- ☐ Tie canvas tops or covers firmly to keep them from ripping in the wind.

- ☐ Make sure that all tie-downs are fastened securely.

- ☐ Check trailer tail lights, stop lights and turn signals.

- ☐ Make sure the hitch is seated and locked, and that the safety chain is crossed under the trailer tongue.

- ☐ Check trailer tire pressure.

Tips for Towing

Since a car with a trailer is slower to accelerate, leave extra room when pulling into traffic or passing other cars. Because of the weight it will also take longer to stop, so anticipate braking situations. Quick starts and stops are hard on the tow car, and sudden turns may cause the trailer to weave from side to side.

Make wide turns. A trailer needs a wider arc to go around street corners than a car. If you cut a turn too tightly you'll find the trailer bumping over the curb. Trailers are also vulnerable to crosswinds or drafts from passing trucks, which can cause the rig to sway. If the swaying is alarming, don't brake. Braking can increase the whipping. Ease your foot off the accelerator and let the car slow down naturally to a comfortable speed. The swaying will stop.

On long trips stop regularly to double-check the tie-downs, the boat and the trailer.

Tips for Backing

Back the car slowly. Very little steering wheel movement will put the trailer where you want it. Oversteering can put you into a jackknife. If the trailer gets too far out of line, simply pull forward to straighten it out and start over.

One way to remember which way the trailer will go is to hold the steering wheel at the bottom. If you move your hand to the right (turning the wheel counterclockwise), the back of the trailer will move to the right. If you move your hand left (clockwise), the trailer will move left.

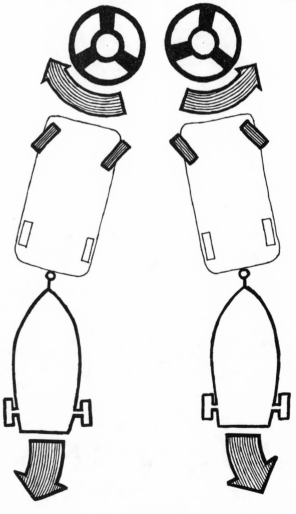

Trailering Drills

As you practice backing up with your trailer, don't think that you can only use reverse. Professional truck drivers, faced with much longer trailers than boatowners, often drive forward slightly to straighten out a trailer that wants to jackknife to one side. Driving a few feet forward can quickly put you back in control of the rig. To prevent loss of control in reverse, go slowly and don't oversteer.

Cornering

Choose an empty parking lot and use a number of large, empty cardboard boxes as markers.

First, construct a "corner" out of the boxes. Make right and left hand turns around it to learn the turning radius of your trailer. This will help prevent you from making mistakes on real street corners.

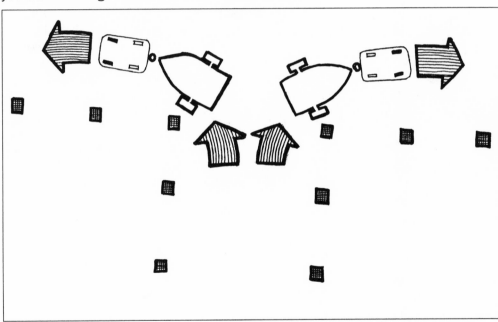

Backing

Next, create a "parking slot" by lining up boxes in two rows, about five feet from each side of the trailer. Drive straight ahead for 50 feet and stop. Then practice backing up into the parking place between boxes. This gives you a feel for how little movement is needed to steer the trailer. To gain confidence try this at increasing distances of 100, 200 and 300 feet. This will enable you to back up straight down the launching ramp.

Trailering Drills

Having a crew member to guide you on the launching ramp can be a great help, particularly if your boat obstructs your rear view. A crew member's simple hand signals, such as a clenched fist to stop or a finger pointing in the direction the trailer should go in, can take the strain out of launching. And, once on the ramp itself, it is helpful to have a crew member signal when you've backed down far enough to launch.

Parking

The final drill will be to back the trailer into the space between the boxes as though you were backing around a corner. Drive the car and trailer at right angles to the boxes, about 40 to 50 feet away from the boxes and to the left of them. By turning the wheel clockwise, you will start the trailer turning toward the parking place. Once you've started the turn, straighten the wheel and the trailer will gracefully arc between the boxes. You'll need practice to determine how far away to stop the trailer and how much to turn the wheel, but you'll become comfortable with the maneuver.

As a final test, you might want to try backing the trailer from the right of the parking place. This is more difficult because you can't see as well. You may want a crew member to help guide you.

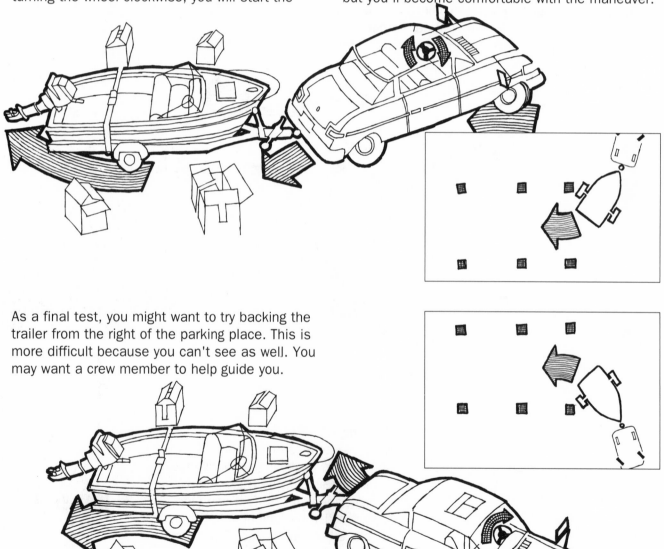

Chapter 3

Second Day Out

Practice Drill #1: Throttle Control

One of the most important elements in operating your boat in a seamanlike manner is the proper use of throttle and shift control. There is seldom any need for heavy use of throttle and shift during maneuvers such as docking. A light touch and smaller amounts of each achieve the same results with less fuss and noise. It goes without saying that bumping into things at slow speed causes less damage.

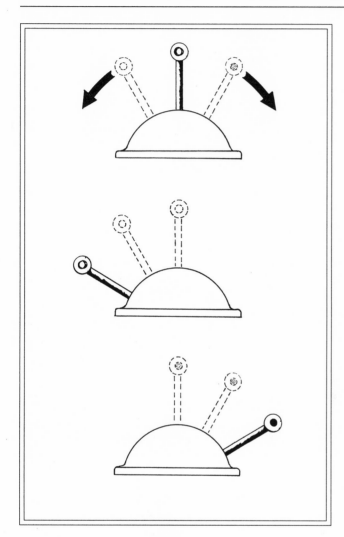

Preparation: Familiarize yourself with the throttle-shift movements with the engine off. Also examine your engine or boat manual for tips on using the throttle and shift aboard your boat. Many small powerboats combine gearshift and throttle into a single-lever control. To prevent accidentally selecting reverse, a button in the shifter may need to be pushed before reverse can be used.

Drill: With the engine running in neutral, push the shift lever forward until you are in forward. Make a note of how far you have to move the lever. Do the same for reverse. These will give you the minimum of power in each gear, which will be used for docking and low-speed maneuvering.

In forward gear, advance the throttle slightly, and see how much speed you have gained. Continue testing up to full speed. Repeat the same procedure for reverse gear and, again, note how much throttle is needed for each amount of reverse thrust. Be careful not to swamp the cockpit.

Using a buoy in open water as a starting point, practice going backwards and forwards so that you can operate the throttle without looking. In many situations, you'll want to rely on the "feel" of the throttle because you'll need to be watching somewhere else.

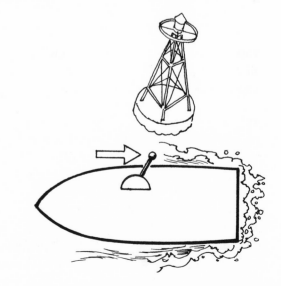

Practice Drill #2: Stopping Distance

Just as important as being able to throttle and shift without looking is becoming aware of the distance needed to come to a full stop. On land, the brakes on a car are highly efficient. On the water, with a little practice, you'll learn to stop very quickly with good control by putting your boat in reverse. At slow speeds, you can count on water friction, current and/or wind to slow you down or stop you.

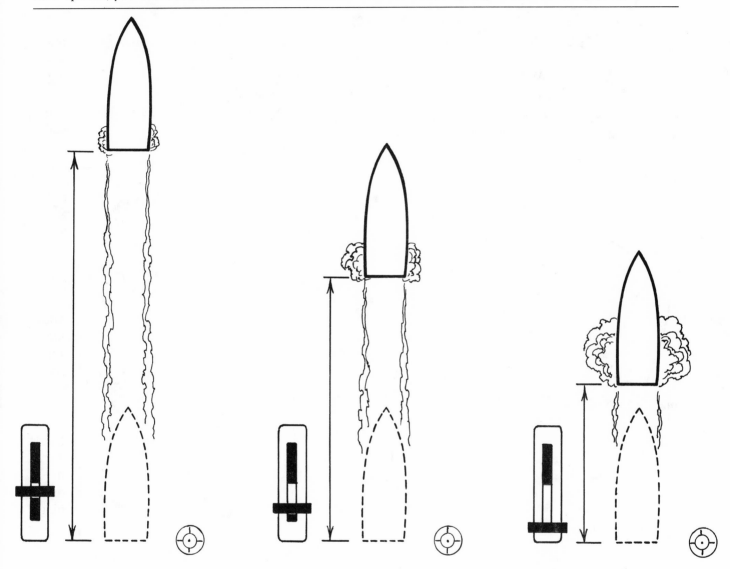

Preparation: Using the same buoy as before, you will be learning how much distance is required to stop your boat at different speeds.

Drill: At idle speed, steer the boat in a straight line past the buoy. As soon as the stern passes the buoy, put the engine in neutral, then reverse at idle speed. By watching the water nearby, you can judge when the forward motion of the boat has stopped. At that point, put the engine in neutral and check the stopping distance. Make another pass at idle speed but use more throttle in

reverse; again note the distance required to stop. Try the same drill at a variety of throttle settings.

Full-power reverse is used mainly in emergencies only since it strains the boat, engine and crew.

Conclusions: At low speeds, very little throttle in reverse is needed to stop your boat, so there is no need to race your engine while docking. As your speeds increase, more power is needed to stop the boat quickly. Note that the more reverse is used, the less control you have over the boat.

Practice Drill #3: Turning

Turning drills are one of the best ways to learn how to handle a new powerboat properly, whether you're a novice or a seasoned seaman. When you buy a new car, it takes time to learn how tightly it will turn and how quickly it will accelerate or stop. The drills on these pages will help you understand your boat's characteristics and illustrate the differences in its turning radius between right and left turns.

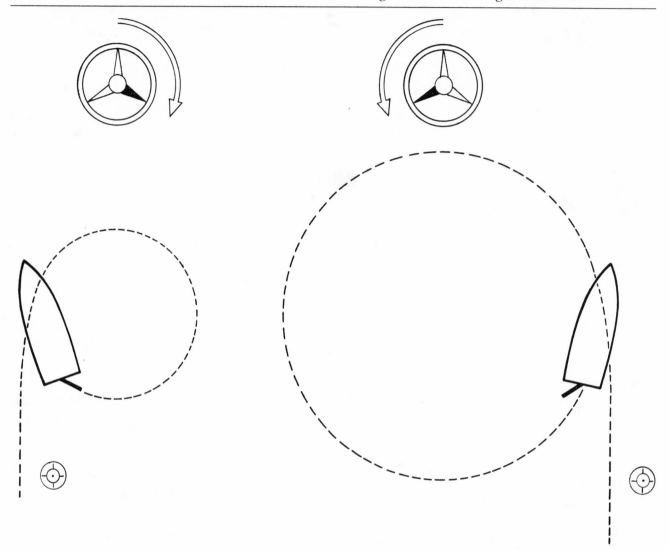

Preparation: Find a floating marker or buoy in an area of smooth water where you can maneuver freely at low and medium speeds without getting in the way of other boats. Using the buoy as a starting point, you'll see how your boat turns in each direction.

Drill: At idle speed, pass close with the buoy on your right side. As soon as your stern clears the buoy (and without changing the throttle), turn the boat hard to the right. As you complete the circle, notice your turning radius. Repeat the drill by turning to your left side.

Conclusions: Most single-engined powerboats have "right-handed" propellers, that is propellers that turn clockwise. Boats thus powered will turn more quickly to the right than to the left. Outboards and sterndrives will have even smaller turning circles than inboards because the thrust of the propeller is actually turned rather than simply deflecting water past a rudder. By looking at the path of your wake, you will notice that you have not made a perfect circle. This is due, in part, to the fact that there is a delay between throwing the wheel over and the boat's response to the new rudder angle.

Practice Drill #4: Circling

It may have been surprising to learn that your boat turns more efficiently in one direction than the other. You will also find that higher speeds produce different turning results. In general, the faster you go, the larger the turning circle. Unlike your car, which has good adhesion, your boat will slip sideways as it turns. At a dead stop, with the rudder hard over, a short burst of throttle will kick the stern to the side.

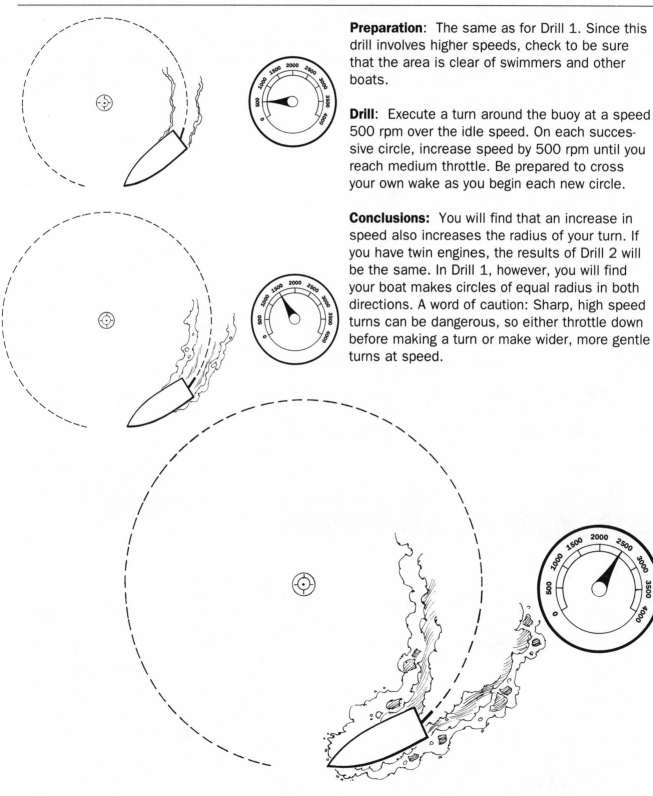

Preparation: The same as for Drill 1. Since this drill involves higher speeds, check to be sure that the area is clear of swimmers and other boats.

Drill: Execute a turn around the buoy at a speed 500 rpm over the idle speed. On each successive circle, increase speed by 500 rpm until you reach medium throttle. Be prepared to cross your own wake as you begin each new circle.

Conclusions: You will find that an increase in speed also increases the radius of your turn. If you have twin engines, the results of Drill 2 will be the same. In Drill 1, however, you will find your boat makes circles of equal radius in both directions. A word of caution: Sharp, high speed turns can be dangerous, so either throttle down before making a turn or make wider, more gentle turns at speed.

Practice Drill #5: Backing

You've already discovered that propeller rotation affects your boat's turning radius in one direction more than the other. You'll discover through this drill that your boat's backing characteristics are also affected by the propeller's rotation. In general, the common right-handed propeller will make your stern move to the left as you back up. This will be true regardless of engine system.

Preparation: A buoy in open water can be used for the first drill, but a more ideal situation would be to find a pier in deep water to serve as a "straight line" for the backing practice outlined in the second drill.

Drill: In open water, duplicate the turning radius tests in reverse and at low speed. You will find that your powerboat will turn much more quickly in one direction. Note this fact for future maneuvers.

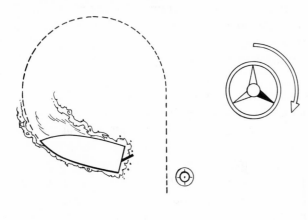

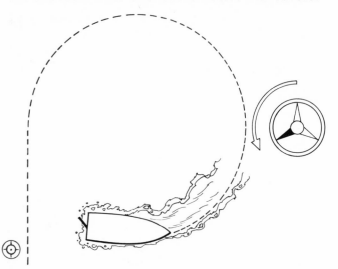

Drill: With the boat parallel to the pier and at a distance of at least two boat lengths from it, put the engine in reverse at idle speed. Start with the drive unit or rudder centered, as though you were proceeding straight ahead. Without turning the wheel, note that the stern will swing in one direction, usually to the left. Try the same drill at a slightly higher engine speed, and note that this increases the tendency of the stern to back to one side.

Stop, realign your boat and again put it in reverse at idle speed. This time, turn the wheel so that the boat backs up in a straight line, and note the amount of turn that is required to compensate for the natural tendency to turn left in reverse.

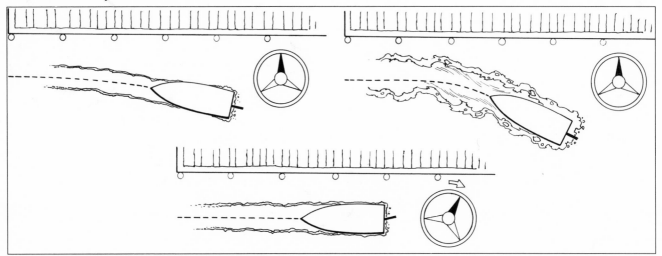

Practice Drill #6: Retrieving Objects

A basic maneuver for small powerboats is to return to a previous spot in order to retrieve something from the water. This can be as common an occurrence as picking up a waterskier or retrieving a hat that blew off. It can also be as crucial as recovering someone who fell overboard accidentally. These are simple maneuvers. Nevertheless, the precision with which they are executed is the result of practice.

Preparation: For your in-water object, use a floating life preserver or a boat fender without a line tied to it so that it won't snag your propeller. Practice this drill in an open water area with calm winds so that the floating object won't blow away.

Drill: Toss the cushion overboard. As soon as it hits the water, turn the boat toward the cushion. This will turn the stern away from the cushion, thus protecting it from the propeller. If there *is* a wind, maneuver to the cushion from downwind. This keeps the boat from being blown down on the object when you stop your engine to retrieve it. If possible, retrieve the cushion on the side nearest the skipper for best visibility.

Retrieving a Person in the Water: You may want to use a thrown line to pull them toward the boat instead of maneuvering close by and thereby risking collision. In either case, be sure that your engine is in neutral or stopped as you near the person so that the propeller is not a threat.

Practice this drill in different wind and wave conditions to determine how your boat is affected in each situation.

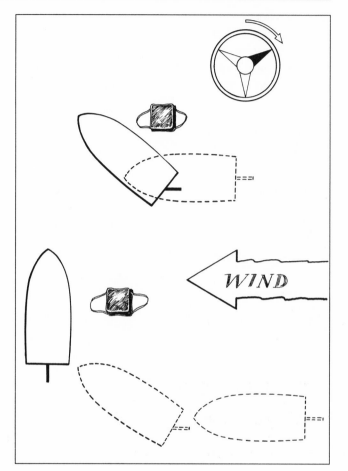

Practice Drill #7: Touch and Go Docking

Just as pilots practice "touch and go" landings to hone their skills, the powerboat skipper should perfect his docking technique practicing with the same method. This is best done at a deserted pier so that you won't get in anyone's way (or be embarrassed by your own early efforts). After a few passes at the pier, you'll soon be confident that you can handle your boat properly in most docking circumstances.

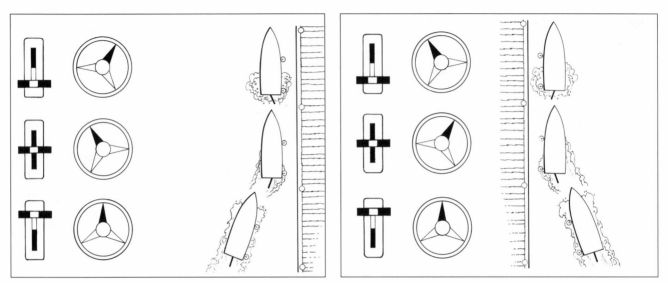

Preparation: The intent is to be skillful enough to bring your boat alongside the dock without relying on the dock lines to pull you into position. Start your practice session early in the day when wind and water are calmest. Hang fenders over the side you plan to dock on.

Drill: Locate a spot on the pier as your eventual destination. Approach the pier at about a 20° angle. Use steering and reverse to align the boat at the pier. As soon as the boat has stopped in the position you desire, move the boat away from the dock and start again. Try approaching port and starboard sides to acquaint yourself with your boat's handling characteristics in close quarters.

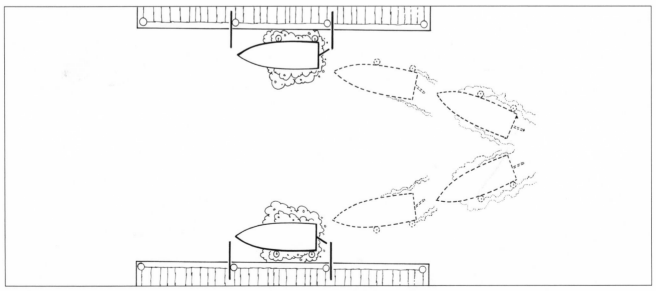

Drill: To practice an approach to a crowded dock, tie broomsticks to the dock, extending out over the water, to mark the space between other "boats." Try several approaches, making sure that you stay within the space you have allotted yourself without touching the neighboring "boats."

Practice Drill #8: Picking Up a Mooring

Although most boat handling skills are used while actually docking, the popularity of moorings in many areas will require you to develop techniques for picking up a mooring float. This procedure is similar in many ways to retrieving a floating object. A little practice with an actual mooring in an isolated area will insure that you know all the steps when you need them in a crowded anchorage.

Preparation: Find an unused mooring buoy. A navigational buoy is not a good substitute. Most moorings have either a ring or a shackle attached to the floating buoy. You'll need a bow line to thread through that eye. Some moorings may already have a line attached so be careful not to tangle your prop as you approach.

Drill: The safest and most controlled approach to a buoy is from the downwind side. Before beginning your approach, locate the wind direction by looking for flags or smoke in the area. Other boats will be downwind of their moorings.

Have the boathook and bow line ready, with someone on the bow to handle the actual tie-up. At idle speed, approach the buoy and, when it is out of sight under the bow, have your crew tell you where it is located. If necessary, the crew can use the boathook to snag the buoy and pull it in. As soon as that's done, put the engine in neutral so as not to run over it. Pass the bow line through the buoy eye and fasten the end to your bow cleat.

If you are alone, you may want to secure the bow line and bring the tail back near the steering wheel. You can then bring the boat alongside the mooring buoy and thread the line from the cockpit.

To depart from a mooring, start your engine, release the end of the bow line and pull it through the buoy eye. Back away from the buoy.

Waterskiing

More than 14 million Americans enjoy waterskiing each year, making it one of the most popular water-borne sports. But there's more to it than just having a boat and finding a deserted body of water. For maximum pleasure and safety the boat should be properly outfitted and the skipper must understand what skills are required. An observer facing aft, toward the skier, must be as involved as the skipper.

Equipping the Waterski Boat
The waterski boat should have a sturdy method of attaching the waterski tow rope. For most boats, this is a bridle attached to two towing eyes on the stern. A rearview mirror can help the driver, and a boarding ladder makes it easier to retrieve the skier. The standard tow line is a 75-foot polypropylene line that floats, with a padded and floating handle. All skiers should wear a flotation device such as the lightweight waterski PFD.

Driving the Waterski Boat
Pick a course in smooth water that is clear of other boats, swimmers and other skiers. If other skiers are in the area, avoid following them in case they fall. Unless the skier is experienced, advise him to stay in the wake of the boat.

Water Starts
With the skier well away from the boat the observer throws him or her the tow line. After double-checking to make sure that the skier is safely away from the boat and that the ski line is clear of the propeller, move the boat ahead at idle speed to take up the slack. When the skier is ready and shouts "In gear!" idle forward to take up the remaining slack. At the skier's shout "Hit it!" the boat should accelerate smoothly up to a speed suitable for the skier's experience level.

In addition to equipping the boat properly, both the driver and the observer should be familiar with the universal waterski hand signals used by the skier to communicate. Equally important is knowing how to retrieve a waterskier from the water quickly or getting the tow line back to a downed waterskier before he or she tires. The observer should watch the waterskier at all times. The driver should look ahead.

Returning the Tow Line

When a waterskier falls, return immediately to the skier's area. Hold one arm up to warn other boats that there is a skier in the water. Make a circle that sharpens after passing the skier. This will drag the tow line past the skier who can grab it and slide back to the end before starting the ski sequence. This should be done at slow speed.

Retrieving the Skier

After circling back and pulling in the tow line, make a slow approach from downwind at idle speed, keeping the skier in sight on the driver's side of the boat. As the boat nears the skier, shift into neutral or turn the engine off while the observer puts the boarding ladder over the side and helps the skier into the boat.

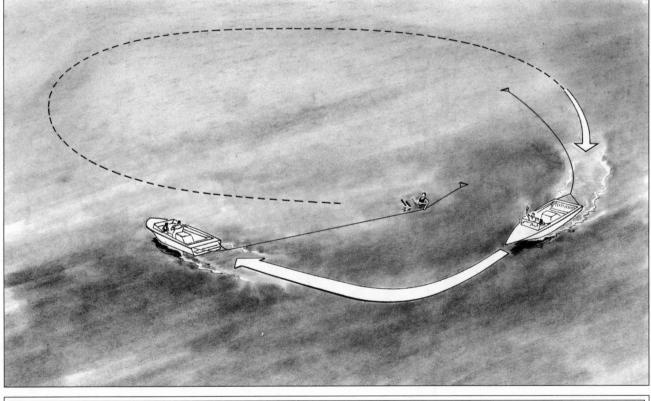

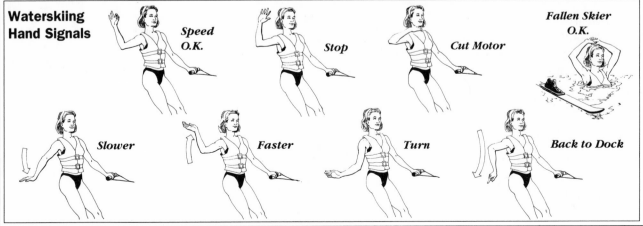

Waterskiing Hand Signals

Speed O.K.

Stop

Cut Motor

Fallen Skier O.K.

Slower

Faster

Turn

Back to Dock

Basic Navigation

Coastal piloting, or piloting, is basically the art of getting from here to there without going aground or getting lost. It requires a few basic tools—a compass, a chart, parallel rules, dividers, a sharp pencil—and a few simple, easy to learn skills. This kind of basic wayfinding allows you to range far afield, venturing out of familiar home waters and into new cruising grounds with a sense of confidence.

TOOLS

Compass: The most basic and useful navigation aid available, the compass houses a card that is magnetically oriented towards north, regardless of your boat's direction. The card reads in degrees. Your boat's heading is indicated by a "lubber's line," a pin or stripe lined up on the clear dome. A professional should adjust the compass to compensate for the magnetic field set up by your boat.

Compass Rose: Taking its name from the flower it resembles, a compass rose on a chart shows two sets of bearings: the outer ring is oriented to true north, while the inner one shows magnetic bearings oriented to the magnetic north pole. Since your compass is magnetically oriented, use the rose's inner (magnetic) bearings for navigational purposes.

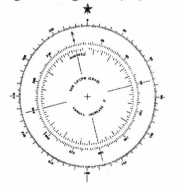

Parallel Rules: This handy device allows you to draw a course between two points, then "walk" the course over to a compass rose to determine the magnetic direction in which to steer.

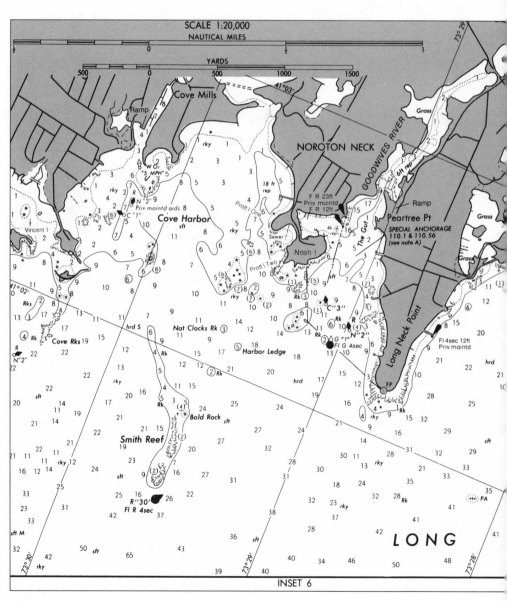

A course on the water, much like a road on land, may not provide the straightest line to your destination. It will, however, take you around or away from shallow areas, land masses, rocks, sunken wrecks and other underwater obstructions. Calculating your route through inland waters and along coastlines also provides a way by which you can recheck and update your current position along the way.

Dividers: Hinged to open or contract, dividers are used to measure distances on charts. Normally, navigational distances are measured in nautical miles (approximately one-seventh longer than statute miles). Speed, in nautical miles per hour, is expressed as knots (not knots per hour).

PLANNING AND STEERING A COURSE

1. Beginning with your starting point, pick your first intended waypoint on the chart. In the example to the left you are starting at N "2" (Nun number 2) and headed for N "24" (Nun number 24).

2. Using the parallel rules and a sharpened pencil, draw a line between the two points.

3. "Walk" the rules over to the center of the compass rose. Do this by holding one rule down firmly while opening the other in the direction of the compass. Then reverse the procedure until one rule bisects the cross lines at the center of the compass.

4. Note where the rule intersects the inner (magnetic) circle in the direction you wish to go. In this case, the indicated course will be 147°.

5. Mark the course on the original line you drew.
Precede the bearing with the letter "C" (for course) and follow it with the "M" (for magnetic).

6. Align the lubber's line on your boat's compass on 147 and try to steer that course.

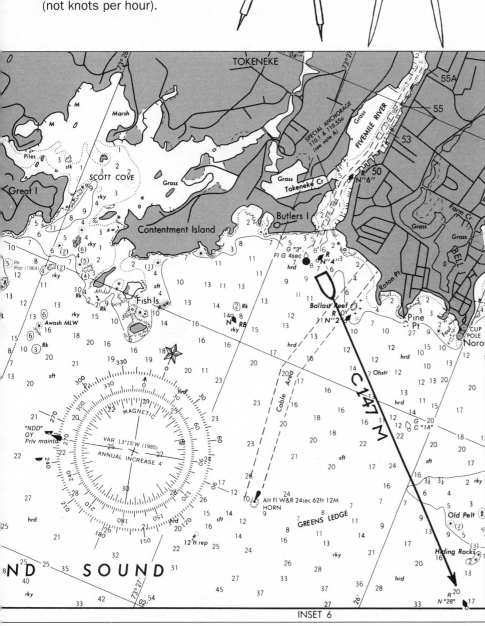

Plotting

Having marked the courses between buoys, the "legs" of your intended trip, you will want to measure them. And, having measured them and added them up for total mileage, you will want to figure out how long it will take to make the trip. Since distance divided by speed equals time, you will first have to learn how to tell boat speed. If you know your speed and distance on a leg, you can compute time in hours.

Course

Examine the chart to determine the best way to get from your departure point to your destination. You may be able to go straight between the two. More likely, however, the trip will require several doglegs to avoid shallow area and hazards. Using a pencil and parallel rules, draw straight lines between the navigational aids you plan to use along the way.

In the example at right, getting from point A to point B requires skirting a reef, peninsula and small island.

Distance

At the top of the chart is a scale in nautical miles. Using the dividers, determine the distance of each leg. Write the distance for each leg beneath the course marked on the line, followed by the letters "nm" (short for nautical miles).

In the example, the first leg is .75 nm, the second is 2.45 nm, the third is .35 nm.

Speed

A tachometer can be used to determine a vessel's speed through the water. Thus, at any given engine rpm, the skipper knows what speed the boat is making.

To come up with a speed table,

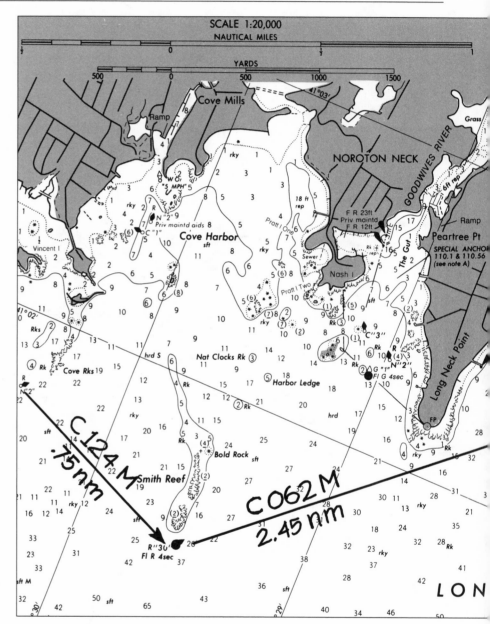

choose a mile-long course between two known navigational aids (e.g., between the horn and nun buoy on the chart above). Run the course each way at a given throttle setting, then do it again and again at increasingly higher settings. Average the time it takes to cover the distance at each setting, convert the average into seconds and divide the seconds into 3,600 (seconds in an hour) to get speed. If the measured mile is a statute (land) mile, speed will be in mph. If the measured mile is a nautical mile, speed will be in knots.

There are various ways to determine boat speed. Some vessels have speedometers. Larger ones are equipped with navigational devices, such as loran, which compute speed electronically. Smaller boats can calculate velocity by timing their running time on a measured mile at different engine rpm. To minimize the effects of wind and tide, timed runs should be made in each direction at a given rpm.

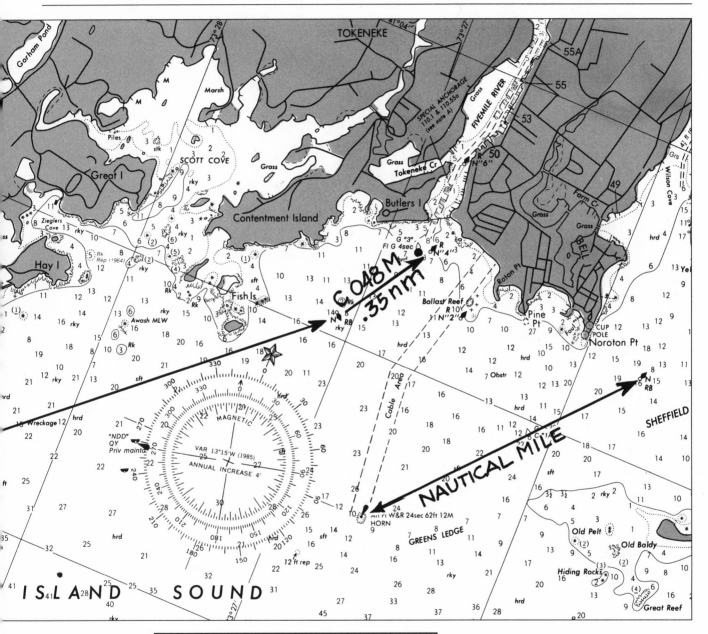

Speed Table

rpm	East-West Time	Speed	West-East Time	Speed	Average Speed
600	9:02	6.6	9:06	6.5	6.5
1,000	7:08	8.4	7:12	8.3	8.3
1,500	5:16	11.4	5:22	11.1	11.2
2,000	3:08	19.2	3:18	18.2	18.7
2,500	2:28	24.3	2:36	23.1	23.7
3,000	2:04	29.0	2:18	26.0	27.5
3,500	1:44	34.6	1:48	33.3	33.9
4,000	1:30	40.0	1:32	39.1	39.5

Dead Reckoning

On long legs between known navigational aids it is difficult to know your exact location at all times. However, by keeping track of your compass course, time and speed on each leg, you can "reckon" where you are at any given moment. Constantly updating your estimated position isn't as necessary in familiar waters as in unfamiliar ones. But knowing where you *should* be is critical in any emergency.

Waypoint

Dead reckoning involves recordkeeping. Each time you pass a waypoint, for example, you should pencil in the time next to it on the chart. If you know your compass course and speed from that point, you can determine your location at any given time along the leg that you are traveling by multiplying your speed by the time that has elapsed since you passed the last waypoint divided by 60 when dealing in minutes. You should also be able to predict your arrival time at the next waypoint (e.g., if you departed Nun "4" at 0935 at a speed of 10 knots, you should arrive at the next nun in about two minutes and at the the red flasher 14 to 15 minutes after that).

Checkpoints

Dead reckoning information should be updated as frequently as possible.

To check your progress on a two-and-a-half-mile leg (the long one on the chart at right), you should note the time you came abreast of Long Neck Point.

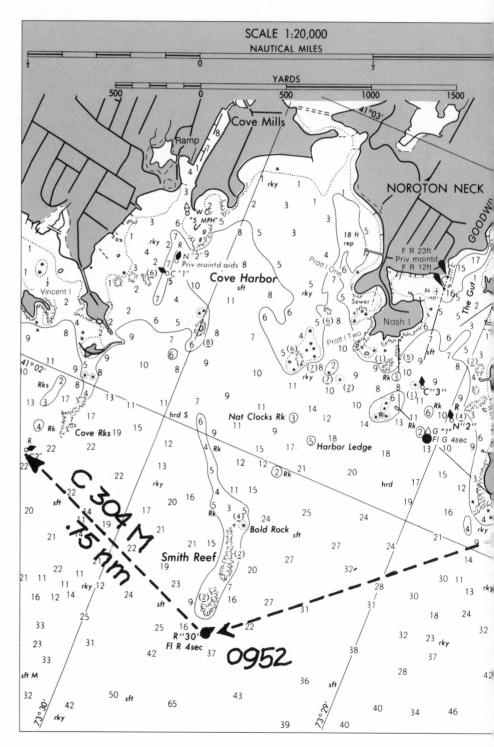

On a long leg of a journey, tides and currents, even wind, may push you off course, slow you down or speed you on your way. The longer the leg, the greater the possibility of deflection. One way to correct and update your dead reckoning is to use waypoints along the way to check your progress on each leg. Look for conspicuous landmarks along the shoreline, nearby headlands and well-defined land contours.

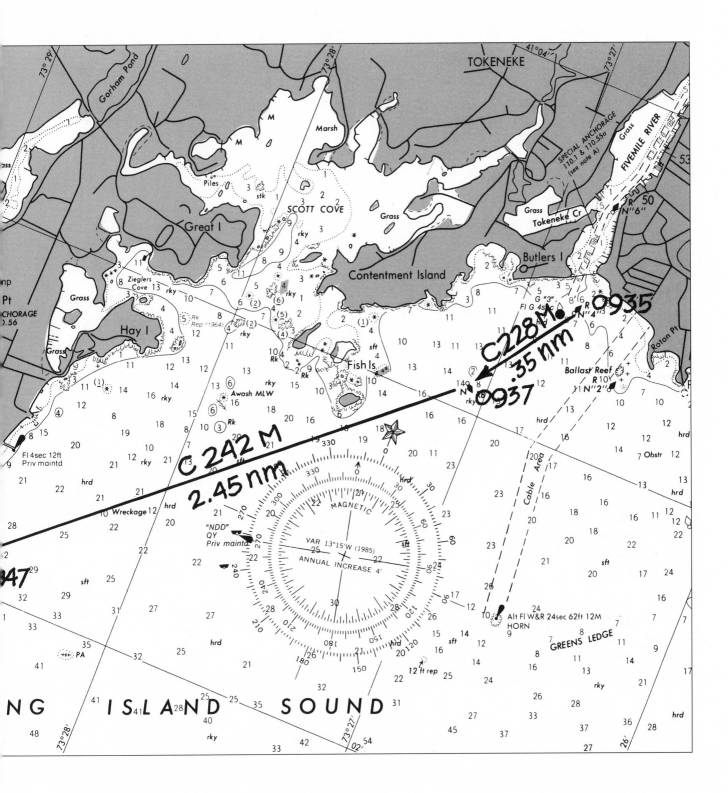

Anchoring

One of the important skills to master if you plan to cruise from one area to another is anchoring. While there is no one anchor or method that will cover all situations, the basics of anchoring so that your boat doesn't drag or endanger other boats are fairly straightforward. Anchoring requires some practice. Do anchoring exercises so that you are proficient enough to anchor in the dark if you ever need to.

Types of Anchors

The most common anchor among small power-boats is the Danforth, or "lightweight" type, since it stores easily and holds well in mud and sand. It is less effective on rocky or grassy bottoms. The folding anchor is good in mud or rock but less effective in sand. Choose an anchor for the bottom conditions in your intended anchorage.

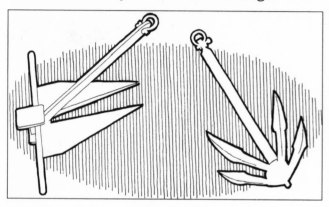

Anchor Rode

The anchor line, or rode, should be a 3/8-inch twisted nylon rode for powerboats up to 24 feet. A length of 3/16-inch galvanized chain, at least 10 feet long, will help the anchor lie flat and hold. Scope is the ratio of anchor line laid out to water depth. For a short stay, 4:1 is an acceptable scope. Any longer or in a blow, use 8:1 or more.

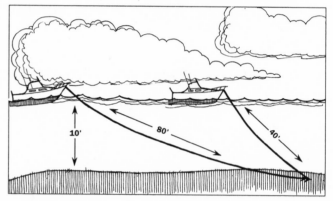

Where to Anchor

Check your chart for water depth and bottom type before selecting your anchorage. If there are other boats at anchor, determine whether they are using a single anchor or are anchored at both bow and stern. If they are using only a single anchor, select a spot that will allow you to swing around in the wind or current without hitting other boats.

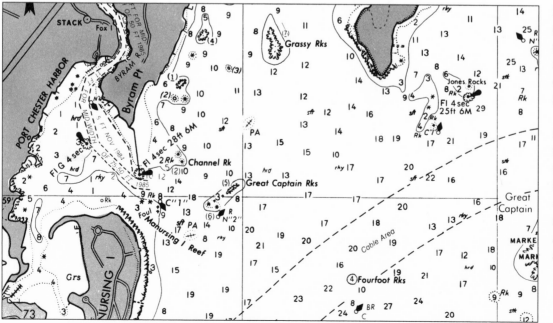

Bottom characteristics are represented on charts by common symbols:

Cl.	clay
Grs.	grass
M.	mud
Rk.	rock
S.	sand
hrd.	hard
rky.	rocky
sft.	soft

Since there is seldom any need to rush through the process, use the same slow, cautious approach to anchoring that you use when docking. After selecting the spot where you want the boat to rest, free the anchor, its chain and rode. Check the shackles to be sure they're snug and make sure that the rode is untangled as you enter the anchorage. Last, make certain that the anchor line end is tied to the boat.

Single Anchor: If possible, use an upwind approach to the area where you want to anchor. Bring the boat to a complete stop and signal to your crew to lower the anchor. Don't throw the anchor over. Lower it gently. When it reaches the bottom the line will go slack. Put the engine in reverse and slowly let out rode. When you have let out the scope you want, secure the anchor line to the bow cleat. Back up slowly under power to help the anchor dig firmly into the bottom. After shifting into neutral, pull on the anchor line. If you feel grating or snatching, the anchor is skimming over the bottom. When the pull is firm and uniform, the anchor is holding.

Weighing Anchor: When you are ready to leave, reverse your anchoring procedure. Power forward while your crew pulls in the anchor rode until the line is vertical. With the engine in neutral, pull up the remaining rode, chain and anchor. Caution: Avoid leaning over to pull up the remaining load. The strain on your back can be enormous. Instead, kneel on deck or squat.

Stuck Anchor: If you can't get the anchor free, secure the rode to the bow cleat and motor slowly ahead. This will pull the anchor rode in the opposite direction of the anchor's set.

Anchoring in Tight Quarters

When you anchor in a narrow channel or in a crowded anchorage where the wind or current is likely to change, use two anchors as shown. The combination will reduce the swinging diameter of your boat and keep you from being pushed ashore when the wind or current changes direction. Be sure that the swinging diameter of your boat does not interfere with other anchored boats or with passage through the channel.

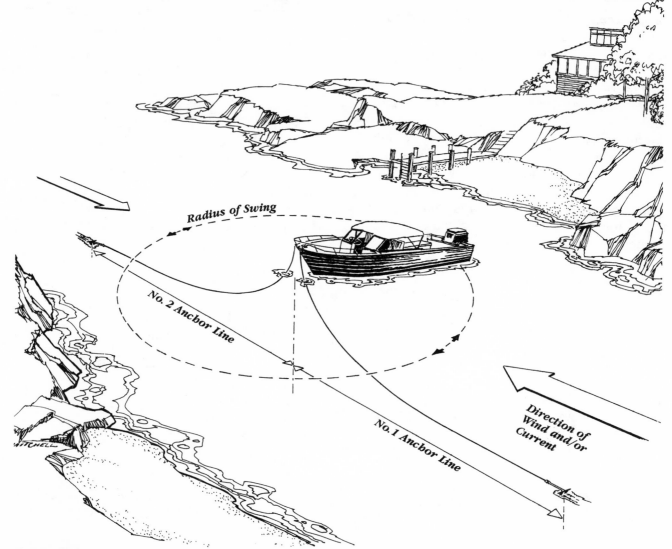

Here's How

• Make your approach into the wind or current, lower your anchor until it reaches bottom and then either drift or power backwards to set it firmly.

• Continue letting out your anchor line as you prepare your second anchor. When you have backed down to the end of your first anchor line, or to the point where you want your second anchor, let it overboard.

• Once the second anchor hits bottom, move back to mid-point between the two. If you have enough crew, you can station one person on the bow to pull in the forward anchor line, another on the stern to let out the second anchor line. You can put the engine in forward to move back to the center.

• With fewer people, you may want to pull the boat by hand back to the mid-point to prevent having the anchor line get caught in the propeller.

• Once you are at the mid-point, secure both lines at the bow so they don't chafe each other.

• To depart, simply reverse the procedure. Let out the upwind or up-current anchor line and drift back over the stern anchor. Once you have the stern anchor up, you can power up to the bow anchor as someone pulls in the slack, and pick it up as well.

Chapter 4

Getting Shipshape

Four Basic Knots

The key to knots and knot tying is knowing how to select the right knot for the job. Some knots are intended to slip easily while others will grow tighter with tension. Your selection should be based on the task at hand. Happily, of the hundreds of knots available to the mariner, a handful will take care of most needs. Nevertheless, your repertoire of knots will grow with your boating experience.

The Bowline is a traditional sailor's knot because it makes a non-slip loop in the end of a line and can be easily undone even after great tension has been applied. A bowline can be used in an emergency to pull someone out of the water since the loop doesn't tighten.

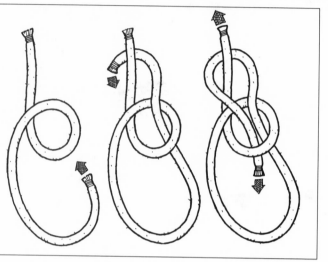

The Square Knot, also called a reef knot, is commonly used to tie lines around an object in order to keep it secure. A symmetrical, flat knot, the square knot is also suitable for joining ropes of equal sizes.

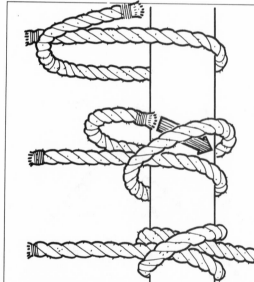

The Clove Hitch will hold as long as there is pressure on it and the source of pressure is in a perpendicular direction to it. On small powerboats, a clove hitch is used to attach dock lines to rails, pilings or bollards on the pier.

Two Half-hitches are a quick way to secure a line that may shift in direction or handle different strain. On a powerboat, two half-hitches are commonly used to hang fenders from handrails. They are also useful for securing lines to mooring rings on docks.

Cleating, Coiling, Stowing and Heaving Lines

Any length of rope (called line on the water) can quickly become a useless snarl unless care is taken to coil it neatly and store it so that it will not tangle. Thus coiled and stowed, a line is ready for instant use. Another seamanlike skill that comes in very handy is learning to throw, or heave, a line so that it reaches its mark. This technique is particularly useful when docking or in emergencies.

Cleating a Line
Lead the end of the line completely around the base of the cleat. Follow this with a crisscross wrap around one horn and finish with a half-hitch on the other horn. The greatest line tension or pull is on the cleat base. The crisscross wrap and half-hitch make the line fast, or secure.

Coiling a Line
Any length of unused line should be coiled so that it's ready for use and doesn't trip you up. Hold the line in your left hand. Feed loops of line in with rhythmic and equal swings of your right hand, giving each section a slight clockwise twist with your fingers to help it form a coil. Braided line, which looks woven, should be allowed to fall into figure-8 coils to prevent kinks.

Stowing the Coiled Line
The best way to stow coiled line on a small powerboat is with a "sea gasket" coil. Take three to four feet of line from the coil. Wrap tightly around the middle of the coil, working upwards. Bring a loop of the remaining "tail" through the center of your coil and slip it over the coil and down. Pull it tight. Your coil will be neatly secured.

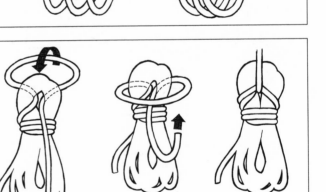

Heaving a Line
Divide the coil of line between your throwing hand and your other hand, which should be kept open. If appropriate, secure the non-throwing end of the line to a cleat. To heave the line, swing your throwing arm back then forward with a strong side-arm movement. The weight of the thrown rope will pull from the coil held in your non-throwing hand. When heaving a line to someone, throw it slightly to one side.

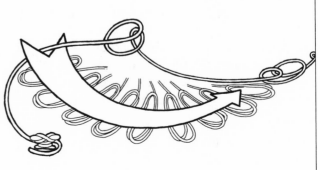

Storage Aboard

No matter how large your boat, finding enough storage will be a constant challenge and you'll soon find you have more items than space to store them in. This gives rise to one of the first rules of boating: "A place for everything and everything in its place." After using an item stow it in its proper place. A corollary rule states "less is more" aboard a boat. Stick to essentials and you'll reduce fuel-guzzling weight.

Food

Since grocery store packaging is bulky, repack your food in Ziploc storage bags in small visible amounts. Canned goods can be tucked under the floor in the bilge, but be sure to remove paper labels beforehand (so they don't clog the bilge pump) and mark the cans with indelible ink. Plastic jugs of water can be frozen at home and used to chill your ice chest until needed. Add dividers or trays to your icebox to make food more accessible. Also, add rice to your salt shakers to keep them from clogging from moisture. Matches and packets of sugar, salt and pepper can be stored in those small plastic containers with watertight lids that are sold in supermarkets. When serving food while under way, a damp towel can serve as a place mat on a dinette or counter to prevent glasses and plates from sliding.

Clothing

Each crew member should have his or her own canvas duffel bag. They stow more easily than suitcases. Large plastic bags can be used for dirty or wet clothing if the duffel bags don't have a lined compartment. Bed linen and blankets can be stored in a spare pillowcase during the day. Small hammocks, sold in marine stores, can be used to store jackets, bathing suits or other clothing against cabin sides.

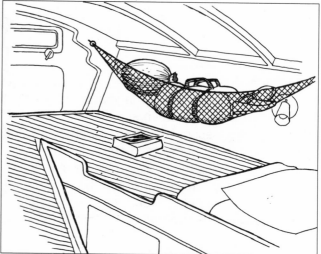

Most small powerboats don't have enough built-in storage space, so you'll need to add your own. Marine hardware stores sell ready-made shelves and lockers that make efficient use of space, or you can simply design your own. Survey the unused space in your boat. Then, when shopping, don't overlook department stores for handy sweater boxes, plastic bins and hanging shelves.

Boat Gear

If you don't have a locker in the bow for the anchor and rode, they can be stowed in a plastic laundry tub tucked under the floor of the cabin until needed. Fishing rods, waterskis, boathooks and paddles can be stowed along cockpit sides in brackets. Tools should be sprayed with anti-rust lubricants and stored in a plastic tool chest. Spare engine parts should also be protected from rust. Fenders and dock lines can be tucked into plastic bins under the cockpit. Or use a bucket which does double duty.

"Fiddles" are the nautical name for rails that keep gear from sliding off shelves and tables. Well-designed boats have them as standard equipment or you can add your own. Shock cords with hooks at each end, sometimes called bungees, are useful to secure boat gear from sliding around. They are available at hardware and marine stores.

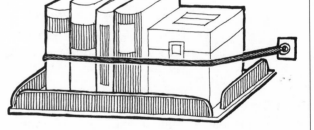

Emergency Equipment

LIfe jackets should be readily accessible in the cockpit lockers or under seats. To keep distress signals accessible and dry, store them in a plastic container with a waterproof cap. On cruising boats, a "grab bag" containing flares, first aid kit, water and other emergency essentials can be stored near the helm.

Weather Tips

For centuries, mariners have relied on their skills at predicting the weather to ensure their safety. Today, the modern skipper has a variety of sources for accurate and up-to-date weather forecasts. Nevertheless, you should pay close attention to local conditions and hone your awareness of ever-changing weather patterns. "Keeping an eye on the weather" is more than just an expression on the water.

Local Weather Forecasts

Detailed current weather information is transmitted continually on four weather (WX) channels on the VHF marine radio. Provided by the National Weather Service, these forecasts are updated every few hours. Additional weather information is available, of course, in newspapers, on radio stations and on television channels. The local airports in many areas maintain a telephone service with recorded weather information.

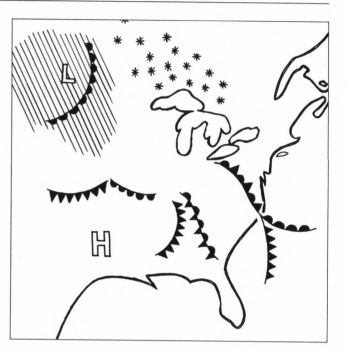

High Front	⊞	Cold Front	▼▼▼▼▼
Low Front	𝕃	Warm Front	⬤⬤⬤⬤
Rain	⧄	Occluded Front	▼⬤▼⬤▼
Snow	✳ ✳ ✳ ✳	Stationary Front	⬤▲⬤▲⬤

Storm Signals

The following visual weather warnings are displayed both day and night in many boating areas:

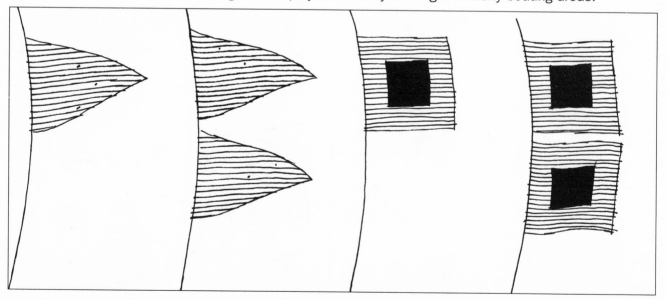

Small Craft Advisory: A single red triangular flag indicates wind speeds from 18 to 33 knots.

Gale Warning: Two red triangular flags, one above the other, indicates wind speeds from 34 to 47 knots.

Storm Warning: A square red flag with a black square in the center, indicates winds 48 to 63 knots.

Hurricane Warning: Two square red flags with black centers indicate winds 64 knots and over.

Local Weather Conditions

While storms generally affect large portions of an area and are usually forecast in advance, the power-boat skipper should be aware of two conditions that can affect his well-being and safety on a more local scale: fog and squalls. Since these weather conditions can be isolated and very localized, they may be unannounced on VHF weather forecasts. The best way to cope with them is to anticipate their arrival.

Fog

Fog is actually a low cloud caused by differences between the air temperature and land or water temperature. The most common fogs on the ocean are advection fogs, the result of warm air flowing over cooler water or land. These usually occur in the summer on northern coastal waters and on the Great Lakes. Steam fog appears more often on rivers and lakes when cool air sinks onto warm waters to produce rising columns of mist. Since fog depends on high humidity to form, keep an eye out for a combination of high humidity, warm wind and cool water. It's a surefire combination, certain to produce fog.

Squalls

A thunder squall may be the forerunner of an approaching cold front or it may be an extremely local storm caused by unstable cool air above a hot land mass. Squalls are unpredictable, can bring winds of gale force and usually appear in hot, humid summer weather. They are marked by fast-moving black cumulus clouds, often with lightning and a line of rain underneath.

Clouds

Clouds are nature's tell-tales, often providing clues to oncoming weather patterns. While there is considerably more to forecasting than simply watching clouds, boatmen have found that the appearance of distinctive cloud types suggest certain weather possibilities. But clouds change constantly, and the skipper who can read the patterns has a decided advantage in recognizing good and bad weather news.

Types of Clouds:
Latin names describe basic cloud types: *Cirrus* **means plumed and feathery wisps;** *Stratus* **means sheetlike; and** *Cumulus* **means heaped.**

Cirrostratus, a high and hazy cloud that causes halos around the sun, usually warns of impending rain or snow.

Cirrocumulus, sometimes called a "mackerel sky," indicates changeable weather.

Altostratus, darker, thicker and lower than cirrostratus, bring rain.

Altocumulus, the traditional cottonball puff clouds of summer, indicate fair weather. Darkening bases can mean light rain.

Cumulus, a fair weather sign, should be watched to make sure it doesn't turn to sudden cumulonimbus and bring thunderstorms.

Nimbostratus is a low dark cloud that often precedes either a cold or warm front and brings steady rain.

If you have trouble distinguishing between one type of cloud and another, don't despair. There are some basic rules for weather. Isolated, wispy or white clouds mean good weather. Dense, dark or tall clouds mean bad weather. And don't forget the old seagoing adage: "Red sky in morning, sailors take warning. Red sky at night, sailors' delight." It can be surprisingly accurate in predicting what's ahead.

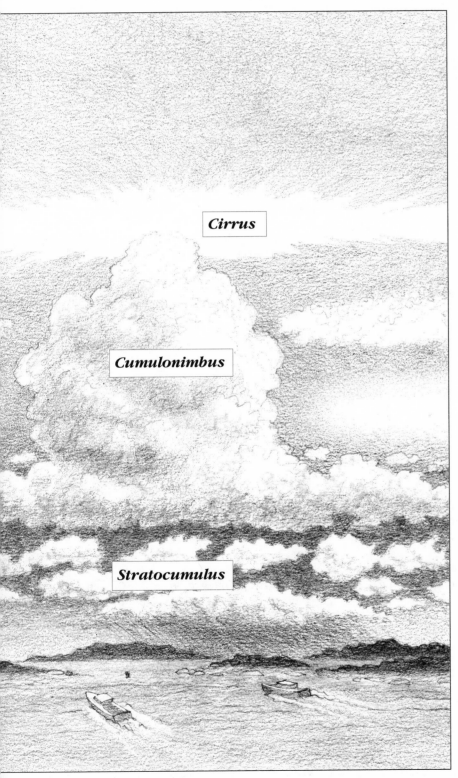

Cirrus

Cumulonimbus

Stratocumulus

Cirrus clouds are high and, moving from the northwest, indicate good weather. But if thick, low clouds appear at the same time, it may forecast rain or drizzle.

Cumulonimbus is the classic thunderhead, bringing wind and rain below.

Stratocumulus clouds in scattered tufts mean good weather but if they join into a solid base, they can bring rain.

Basic Electronics/VHF Radio

A radio lets you communicate with others and it provides a way to broadcast in an emergency. The most common type of radio is the VHF/FM, monitored by the U.S. Coast Guard and used to communicate with other boats, marinas and bridges. In addition, the VHF radio can be linked to land-based telephones for calling friends and businesses. Its range is limited to about 15 miles between boats.

Selecting a VHF Radio
Most radios have 78 or more channels, including Channel 16 which is used in emergencies. More expensive models have scanners that monitor two or more channels, waterproof components and keypad channel entry. You will need a radio station license that provides the call letters for your boat. License forms are available from your dealer, marine electronics store or the local FCC office.

Using the VHF Radio
Channel 16 is used in emergencies and for making contact with other vessels before switching to other channels to converse. When you are out on the water, leave your radio tuned to Channel 16 and adjust the squelch knob so that the static disappears. Safety information, storm advisories and emergencies are often announced on this channel. Weather information is transmitted continuously on one of the WX channels.

Calling Another Boat
• Listen on Channel 16 to see if it is busy.

• State the name of the boat you are calling, followed by your boat name and call sign. You may repeat the call but you must not take more than 30 seconds. Example: "Phaedra, this is Halcyon, WYS 5386."

• Listen for a response and wait at least two minutes before repeating the call.

• After establishing contact on Channel 16, both boats should switch to an agreed upon "working channel" (such as 68, 69 or 71) to free Channel 16 for emergencies. Example: "Phaedra, switch to 71, over."

• The word "over" indicates that you have finished your transmission and are waiting for a response.

• To end a call, give your boat name, call sign and the word "out." Example: "This is Halcyon, WYS 5386, out."

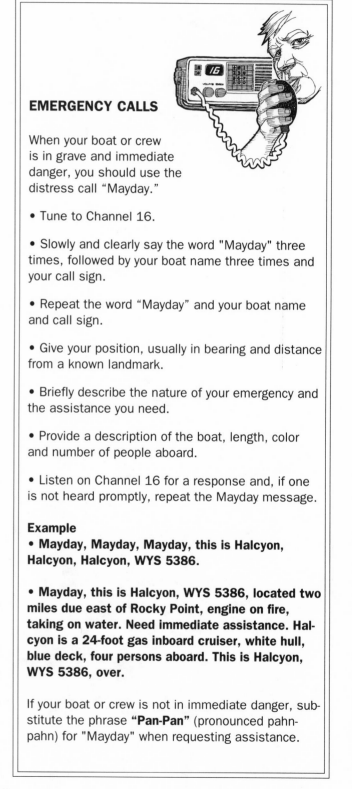

EMERGENCY CALLS

When your boat or crew is in grave and immediate danger, you should use the distress call "Mayday."

• Tune to Channel 16.

• Slowly and clearly say the word "Mayday" three times, followed by your boat name three times and your call sign.

• Repeat the word "Mayday" and your boat name and call sign.

• Give your position, usually in bearing and distance from a known landmark.

• Briefly describe the nature of your emergency and the assistance you need.

• Provide a description of the boat, length, color and number of people aboard.

• Listen on Channel 16 for a response and, if one is not heard promptly, repeat the Mayday message.

Example
• **Mayday, Mayday, Mayday, this is Halcyon, Halcyon, Halcyon, WYS 5386.**

• **Mayday, this is Halcyon, WYS 5386, located two miles due east of Rocky Point, engine on fire, taking on water. Need immediate assistance. Halcyon is a 24-foot gas inboard cruiser, white hull, blue deck, four persons aboard. This is Halcyon, WYS 5386, over.**

If your boat or crew is not in immediate danger, substitute the phrase **"Pan-Pan"** (pronounced pahn-pahn) for "Mayday" when requesting assistance.

Basic Electronics/Sounder

The depth sounder is the second most useful piece of electronic equipment for most small powerboats since it warns of shallow water. Also valuable as a navigation tool, a depth sounder can be used by the skipper to help pinpoint a boat's location by comparing the indicated water depth against soundings on a chart. Some depth sounders have features that allow fishermen to spot schools of fish below the boat.

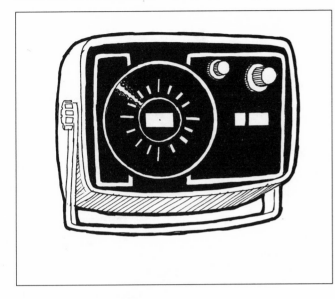

Selecting a Depth Sounder

The most common type of depth sounder in small boats is the digital sounder, which displays the depth as a number.

The flasher sounder, which has an illuminated bulb showing the depth on a clock face, can be used by an experienced skipper to locate fish as well as to determine the suitability of the bottom beneath the boat for anchoring. Most sounders have a feet/fathoms selector, thus offering a way of pairing the selection with the depth indications shown on charts of the area.

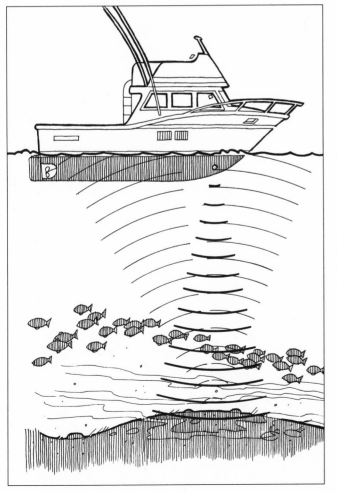

Using the Sounder

With a digital sounder, you simply turn the unit on and keep an occasional eye on the depths.
With a flasher, you tune the sensitivity knob so that the bottom shows as a solid band.
If you plan to fish, you may want to increase the sensitivity so that fish appear as faint flashes between the surface and the bottom.

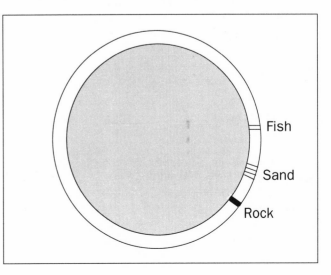

Fish

Sand

Rock

Hull Maintenance/Waxing and Painting

Despite claims to the contrary, fiberglass is not entirely maintenance-free. Although it's considerably easier to maintain than wood, you still should expect to perform routine tasks to prevent fading and chalking of the outer layer called gelcoat, due to exposure to sun and water. If you do it regularly, you'll find that it's much easier than trying to catch up after letting it go too long.

Cleaning the Hull

Regularly washing the boat with fresh water will help keep stains from forming. If the boat is particularly dirty, use a low phosphate liquid detergent, warm water and a soft sponge or cloth. Since mildew grows well in phosphate, be sure to rinse the hull thoroughly after using it.

Cleaning the Deck

Non-slip areas on the deck should be scrubbed with a stiff-bristled brush to lift the dirt out of the pattern. In bad cases, you can use a mild abrasive powder. Do not, however, use the powder on smooth surfaces since it will scratch the finish.

Cleaning Windshields

If your windshield is glass, use a conventional window cleaner. To remove stubborn spots from salt or hard water, use a cloth dipped in vinegar. Plastic windshields and side windows should be cleaned with a plastic cleaner to prevent scratches and hazing. If you do need to remove a scratch, try a commercial scratch remover, or use non-crunchy peanut butter or toothpaste as a mild rubbing compound.

Cleaning Upholstery

There are many vinyl upholstery cleaners available. However, to get mildew out of the creases, mix 1/4 cup of ammonia to 4 cups of water and scrub the crease with a toothbrush or similar brush. Rinse thoroughly afterwards.

Cleaning Fenders

Many solvents, such as acetone, can make a fender or the soft rubrail of a boat sticky, but you can remove dirt and scuffs easily by using a rag soaked in mineral spirits.

Cleaning Iceboxes and Icechests

By the end of boating season iceboxes will sometimes acquire a smell as well as stains from spills. Mix a thick paste of baking soda and water, scour the inside of the box, let it sit for a while, then rinse thoroughly.

CLEANING DECK & HULL	CLEANING UPHOLSTERY
Water	Water
Low-phosphate liquid	Cloths
Detergent	Toothbrush
Sponge	Vinyl Cleaner
Soft-bristle brush	Ammonia

The best way to keep your fiberglass boat in like-new condition is to wax it regularly. First, wash it thoroughly and dry it off with a soft rag. Be wary of cleaner/waxes which can scratch the surface and leave a wax residue. Instead, use a hard marine paste wax on the hull and topsides since auto waxes are not intended to fill the porous surfaces found on fiberglass. Renew the wax once (preferably twice) a year.

Waxing the Hull

The easiest way to wax your boat is to rent or buy an electric buffer. Spread the hard paste wax onto the buffer pad with a stick, then apply it, following directions. When it has dried to a haze, put a clean terry cloth pad on the buffer and bring the hull to a shine. Don't get so far ahead in applying the wax that it becomes hard to remove. If that occurs, apply more wax to soften the earlier coat, then buff it promptly.

Using Rubbing Compound

If your fiberglass has been allowed to weather, it will develop a chalky, dull finish that must be removed with rubbing compound. Start with a mild liquid compound and use a buffer to remove the oxidized surface. Don't let the buffer remain in one place too long or you'll remove too much surface. Keep it moving steadily.

Dealing With Decals

Modern powerboats often use decals and other adhesive panels for styling. Be careful not to use abrasives on them. Some waxes can also cause decals to turn yellow. The best protection is a liquid sealant, used before waxing the hull. Any wax that gets on the decal should be wiped off. Be careful not to buff across the edge of decals because this can cause them to lift. If you do have lifting edges, trim them back gently with a razor or use decal adhesive, available at hobby shops, to reattach them.

Bottom Paint

If you leave your boat in the water, you should coat the bottom with anti-fouling paint which has chemicals to keep barnacles and other growth from adhering. Even freshwater lakes and rivers can cause slime growth. Some modern bottom paints may last as long as three seasons but when they lose their effectiveness they must have any growth removed and be repainted. Outboards and sterndrives must be coated with a special non-metallic paint to prevent corrosion.

WAXING/ COMPOUNDING THE HULL	BOTTOM PAINTING
Automatic buffer	Paint brush
Rubbing compound	Non-metallic paint for sterndrives and outboards
Paste wax	
Soft cloths	Anti-fouling paint for bottom painting

Engine Maintenance

A program of preventive maintenance for your engine can help ensure trouble-free boating. Inboard engines and sterndrives have similar maintenance programs. Regular pre-start checklists, like those used by airline pilots, serve as useful reminders. In addition, you should plan to give your engine a thorough once-over examination every few weeks to check items that aren't part of the pre-start list.

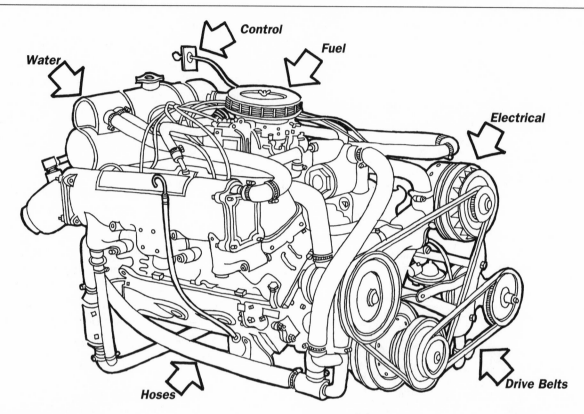

Oil and Water Levels
These should be checked prior to each outing. Plan to change the oil after every 100 hours of running, or sooner if the engine manual recommends it. In addition, squeeze the water hoses. If they feel soft they should be replaced. Rubber tubing dries out quickly in a hot engine compartment. Preservative solutions help prolong hose life. When you buy a hose, get new hose clamps and a spare hose as well.

Drive Belts
These can wear, stretch and develop cracks on the inner surface or break. Always keep spares on board.

Electrical System
A major cause of engine problems is the mixture of moisture and electrical power. Carry spare spark plugs and plug wires, distributor cap and rotor. Water-displacing lubricants help keep moisture out of critical parts.

Fuel System
Check and clean the carburetor fuel filter every two to three months, particularly on outboards. The flame arrestor on the carburetor should be cleaned at the same time. On outboards with portable fuel tanks the rubber fuel hose should be checked for leaks or wear.

Control System
Most shift and throttle cables, as well as steering systems, have lubrication points which can be greased to prevent binding. Your owner's manual will point these out.

Miscellaneous
All hoses should be double clamped for security. Use an engine degreaser to clean the engine so leaks or rust can be spotted. Touch up rust spots with a marine-grade anti-rust paint after sanding the spot down to the bare metal. Also pump out and clean the bilges under the engine to prevent moisture and dirt from getting to the engine.

Drive Unit Maintenance

Since the engines of inboards and sterndrives are generally similar to those found in automobiles, most skippers will be familiar with basic maintenance tasks. The underwater drive units for sterndrives and outboards require a separate program of lubrication and maintenance. These are best performed while doing other routine tasks. Lubrication, however, must be done when the boat is out of the water.

Flushing

The best maintenance for a drive unit is to flush it regularly with fresh water. This can be done by immersing the unit in a drum of water, starting it and letting it idle, or by attaching a garden hose to the water intake with a fitting available at marine dealers. Flushing with fresh water removes salt deposits that can clog the water system. It will also flush out any sand or other materials that can damage the engine's water pump impeller.

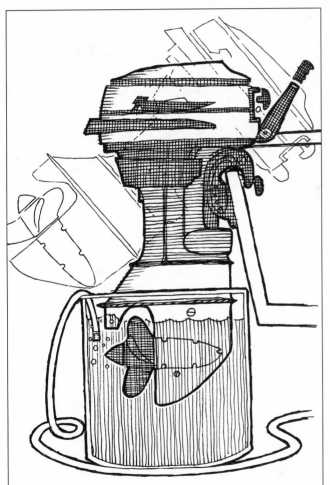

Tilt Mechanism

Outboards and sterndrives have hydraulic tilt mechanisms that move the drive unit up and down. Your owner's manual will show you how to check the hydraulic fluid reservoir level. Do it regularly. At tune-up time you may want to replace the fluid. Look at the seals around the hydraulic cylinders to make sure they aren't leaking.

Exhaust

With the engine tilted up, inspect the accordion-like rubber exhaust hose on sterndrive units for holes caused by wear or barnacles. The hose should be securely clamped in place.

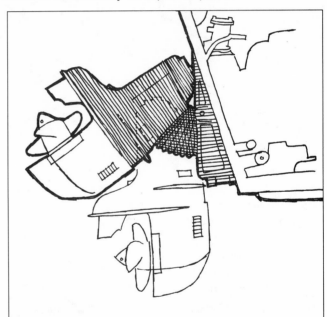

Lubrication

Drive units require regular gearcase lubrication at the front end of the pro-peller housing. The owner's manual will show you how to inject special oil into the unit, and how to check the level.

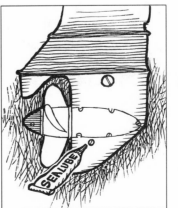

Trailer Maintenance

A trailer seems so simple that many owners forget that they require the same kind of regular maintenance as the boat and engine. If the trailer is immersed at launching, it faces damage from water. Even if it is kept out of the water, it still gets regular baths from the boat and during washdowns. Perform maintenance when the boat is off the trailer. That's when to inspect it for needed repairs.

Boat Supports
If you have pads, the carpeting may decay or tear. It can be replaced easily. Rubber rollers should be checked for ease of turning and lubricated periodically with a spray or grease. Replace any roller that is cracked.

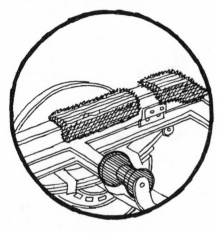

Wheel Bearings
These should be repacked often to prevent rust. If your trailer has sealed bearings, they should have grease injected regularly to keep them filled.

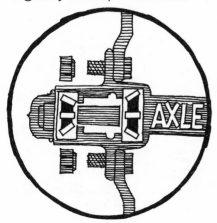

Wheels and Tires
Make sure that the tires are properly inflated when the boat is on the trailer. Check the lugnuts for tightness. Loosen them regularly to keep them from corroding in place.

Hitch
The ball on the car should be removed or covered to prevent rust. The inside of the hitch assembly on the trailer should be greased for easy operation.

Electrical
Trace the wires from the lights to the hitch to check for frayed or worn spots. Repair these with electrical tape.

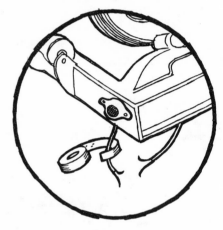

Storage
If you plan to store the boat on the trailer, block the trailer up so that the tires don't develop flat spots. Loosen the tie-down straps so that the hull won't be deformed, and tilt the boat so that any water will drain out.

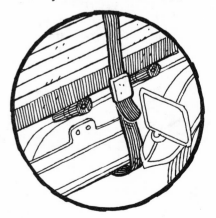

Chapter 5

Handling the Scrapes

Emergency Gear

Simply having emergency equipment on board your boat is not enough. Both you and your entire crew must know exactly where each item is located and how to use it. Even an item as seemingly simple as a life jacket can be difficult to don in a crisis, and there is never time to read the instructions in an emergency. Regular practice sessions can save lives. See pages 26-29 for additional emergency gear.

Life Jacket

Enough life jackets in the proper sizes should be available for the entire crew, and easily accessible from the cockpit. Remove them from their plastic covers, and undo the straps so that they are ready to use. Even though it seems tidy, a vinyl "storage case" for life jackets can be a hindrance in an emergency.

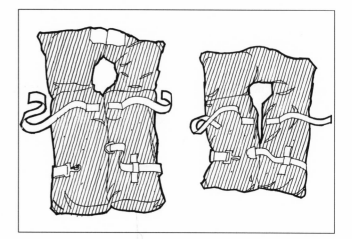

Fire Extinguisher

Each fire extinguisher mounts to a bulkhead differently. Understand how to remove it quickly. Some extinguishers also have a pin that must be removed before it can be used, or a nozzle that must be aimed at the fire. Don't test your extinguisher until needed, however, because you will want full pressure.

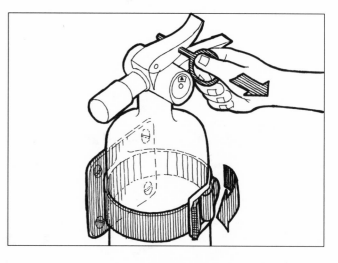

Bilge Pump

The crew should know where the electric bilge pump is located in case you need to clear it if the intake is clogged. A manual pump should also be aboard or, better yet, one or two large buckets with sturdy handles.

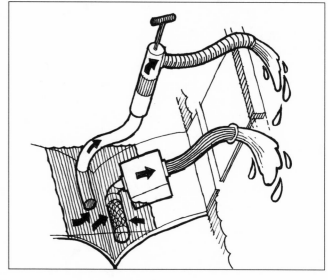

Distress signals, intended to attract help in an emergency, should be stored in a cool, dry spot that is readily accessible at a moment's notice. Since flares burn with great heat, precautions must be taken by anyone who is using them. Aerial flare guns must be registered in some states as firearms. These should always be treated with the same respect accorded to any firearm.

Handheld Flares

These may be ignited by scraping against a rough surface, or they may light when exposed to the air. In either case, hold them by the handle, point the flame away from your body and hold the flare over the side of the boat so that any burning particles fall harmlessly overboard.

Smoke Flares

Ignited like other flares, these should be held at the downwind corner of the boat so that the crew's visibility is not obstructed. Some smoke flares also have hot drippings, so hold them over the side of the boat as well.

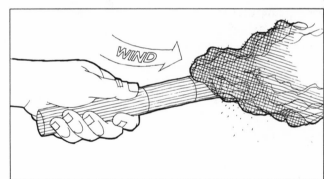

Aerial Flare Pistols

To load the pistol, make sure the hammer is not cocked. Open the barrel while aiming away from the boat. Insert the flare, close and lock the barrel. Cock the pistol by pulling the hammer back. Point the flare up at a 45° angle away from the boat and pull the trigger. Wait a few seconds for the cartridge to cool before reloading. Do not fire a second flare until the first one has completely burned out.

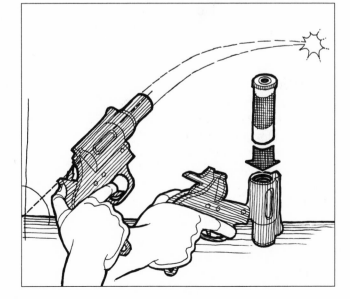

Man Overboard

In many cases, if a member of your crew falls overboard it is not a life-threatening situation since the boat is maneuverable and it is relatively easy to get the person back on board. But the energy-sapping effects of cold water, the difficulty of swimming with soggy clothing or the possibility of injury could turn the situation serious. The swimmer should be retrieved as quickly as possible.

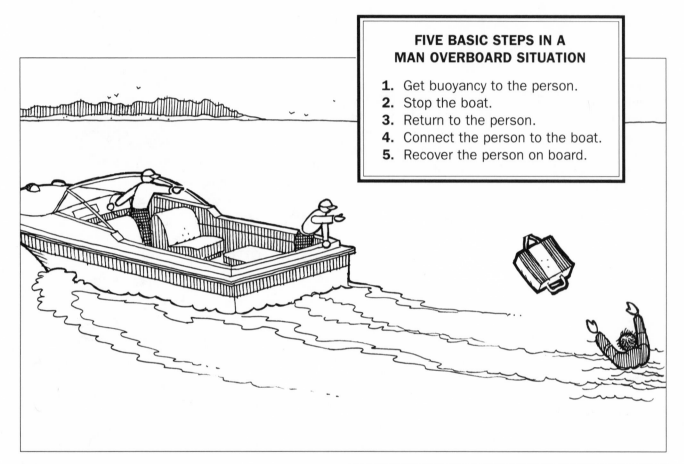

> **FIVE BASIC STEPS IN A MAN OVERBOARD SITUATION**
>
> 1. Get buoyancy to the person.
> 2. Stop the boat.
> 3. Return to the person.
> 4. Connect the person to the boat.
> 5. Recover the person on board.

Buoyancy

As soon as possible, someone should throw a buoyant cushion or life jacket to the swimmer. Keep a Type IV cushion ready in the cockpit for this purpose.

Stopping

Throttle back immediately and have one of your crew members watch the swimmer at all times. In calm water this poses no problem but in rough seas a swimmer's head can be hard to spot. At night, use a flashlight to spotlight the swimmer.

Returning

Approach from the downwind side so you don't drift down onto the swimmer. Plan your approach to keep the swimmer on the driver's side for visibility and have your crew rig a boarding ladder.

When recovering the swimmer, it is important to keep the person close to the boat so that he or she doesn't drift away. A dock line can be thrown to the person for this purpose. On a small powerboat, be sure to maintain proper balance. Your entire crew should not rush to one side of the boat to help in the recovery unless every person is absolutely needed. Calm should prevail throughout the procedure.

Connecting

In the absence of a tethered cushion or life jacket, a dock line with a loop tied in the end can be thrown to the swimmer, to be slipped around the chest to keep the person nearby as the boat drifts with the gearshift in neutral.

Recovery

If the swimmer is in good condition, coming aboard via a boarding ladder is the easiest method of retrieval. Most small powerboats have low sides and even a heavy person can be pulled aboard by members of the crew. If there is no ladder, the engine can be stopped and the swimmer can use the sterndrive or outboard as a step.

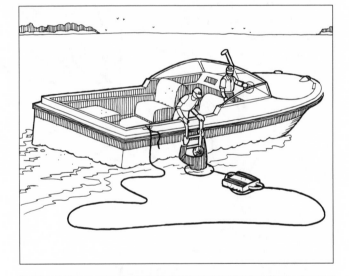

Note

There is often the temptation for a crew member to jump into the water to help the swimmer. This should be avoided unless the swimmer is in trouble since it doubles the number of people to recover. If anyone goes to the assistance of a swimmer, he or she must wear a PFD and be attached to the boat with a sturdy line.

Fires

Since fire on a boat is second in seriousness only to sinking, you want to keep fire-fighting equipment as readily available as the vessel's lifesaving devices. Frequent checks to be sure your extinguishers are properly charged are not wasted effort. Nor are drills in which everyone is made aware of what to do. Speed is of the essence when dealing with a fire aboard; calm and quick action is the best approach.

WHAT TO DO FIRST

1. Have your crew put on their life jackets.
2. Keep the fire downwind of the boat. If the fire is in the stern, turn the boat into the wind. If the fire is forward, turn the boat downwind.
3. Stop the boat to minimize the effect of wind on the flames.
4. If the fire is in loose gear, such as a cushion or pot, throw the burning object overboard.
5. Localize the fire by closing engine hatches or portholes.
6. Close off fuel lines and move portable fuel tanks and flammable material away from the fire area.

Fire-fighting Techniques

With dry chemical fire extinguishers, aim at the base of the fire and squeeze the trigger in short squirts, using a sweeping motion to fan the chemical across the bottom of the fire. Don't wait to see if one fire extinguisher is sufficient. Gather all extinguishers for immediate use. Use the contents of each until you are sure that the fire is extinguished and will not reignite. But save at least part of one in case the fire reignites.

COAST GUARD-REQUIRED CLASS B FIRE EXTINGUISHERS

On the assumption that you will probably have a Class B (gas or grease) fire the Coast Guard requires that you have either a Type B-I or B-II extinguisher on board, depending on boat size. (See page 26.) Dry chemical is the least expensive, carbon dioxide leaves no residue, freon or Halon is usually part of automatic systems and foam is legal but rarely used aboard boats.

Type and Size Classification	Dry Chemical	Carbon Dioxide	Freon	Foam
B-I	2 lb.	4 lb.	2-1/2 lb.	1-1/4 gal.
B-II	10 lb.	15 lb.	——	2-1/2 gal.

Different types of fires require different techniques and materials to put them out. Fire extinguishers are classified by size (I or II) and by the type of fire (A, B or C) they are designed to put out. Water, unfortunately, is of little use in fire fighting on board a powerboat since most fires will be of gas, grease or electrical origin. Dry chemical extinguishers, which can be used on all fires, are the most popular.

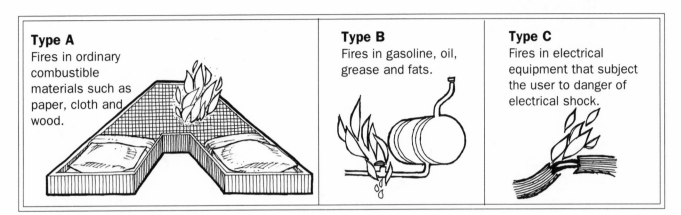

Type A
Fires in ordinary combustible materials such as paper, cloth and wood.

Type B
Fires in gasoline, oil, grease and fats.

Type C
Fires in electrical equipment that subject the user to danger of electrical shock.

Alcohol, Wood or Fabrics

Water can, for the most part, be used to douse fires fueled by wood, fabric or alcohol. Nevertheless, water can sometimes spread an alcohol fire by splashing the alcohol to other areas. Shut off the stove before extinguishing the blaze. Use an appropriate extinguisher.

Grease

Water must not be used on these fires. It is best handled by a Type B extinguisher.

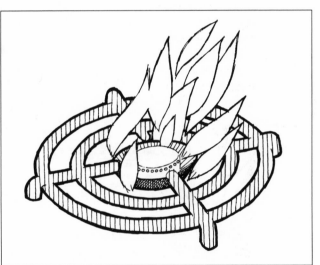

Engine Fires

Immediately turn the engine ignition off and, if possible, shut off the fuel valve. Open the engine cover slightly using a paddle or boathook and shoot the contents of the extinguisher into the engine compartment. Be cautious when re-opening the hatch, as the fire may re-ignite.

Electrical Fires

Cut off the power to the circuit and smother the burning area with Type C chemical. Make sure that the fire is fully extinguished and that nearby materials are not smoldering.

Notes

Aboard a fiberglass boat, you can use water to cool down fiberglass in a fire area. You can also use water to dampen your own clothing and fabrics in the fire area.

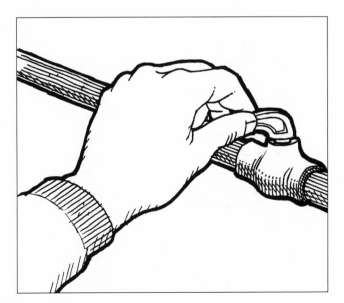

Collision

Although collisions between small powerboats tend to result in minor damage, be prepared to handle the results of more serious crashes. Besides the aspect of personal injury, the major concern is serious damage to the hull, either above or below the waterline, since a hole near there can sink a boat. This kind of damage should be repaired as quickly as possible and excess water removed from the bilge.

WHAT TO DO AFTER A COLLISION

1. Check for injuries among the crew.
2. Locate any leaks.
3. Stop the leak.
4. Heel the boat to raise the damaged part out of the water.

After Collision
If there is water coming aboard, turn on the electric bilge pump and start your crew bailing with buckets while you locate the source of the leak. A flashlight is indispensable for spotting leaks in a dark bilge.

Stopping the Leak
The most common hole in a powerboat is a puncture, the result of hitting another boat or obstruction. If the hole is below the waterline, you can stuff a jacket or blanket into the hole to reduce the flow. These can be wedged in place using a boathook, paddle or even a waterski.

Heeling
Because small powerboats are fairly light, you may be able to stop or slow a leak near the waterline by having the crew sit on the opposite side of the boat. This will heel, or tilt, the boat and raise the damaged part out of the water.

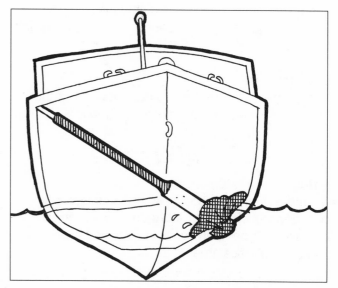

Aside from actual collision, there are certain other situations that may cause water to leak into your boat and you should be prepared to deal with these as well. Loose bolts or fittings can create small leaks. One of the most common leaks occurs when the crew forgets to put in the drain plug in the stern before launching. Again, the most critical aspect of damage control is locating the source of the leak.

Seacocks

Small powerboats may have seacocks, or through-hull fittings, leading to the engine, the marine head and to a galley sink drain. A tapered plug of soft wood, available at marine stores, should be kept aboard to seal these openings if the fitting breaks or the hose leading from it comes loose.

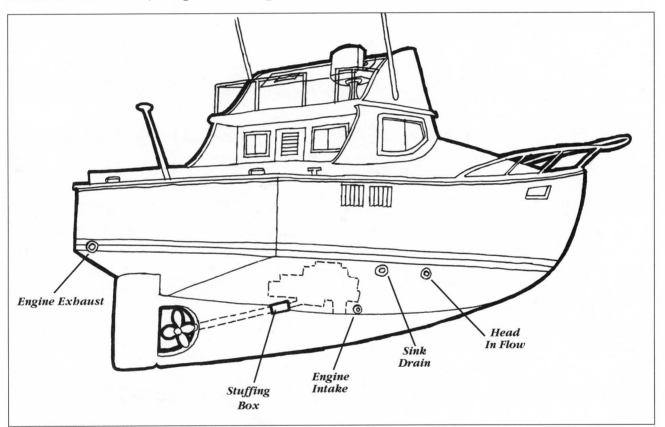

Engine Exhaust

Stuffing Box

Engine Intake

Sink Drain

Head In Flow

LEGAL

Coast Guard regulations require that a boat operator file a report for any incident that involves loss of life, personal injury requiring medical treatment beyond first aid, loss of the vessel, damage to property at a minimum set by each state (usually $100-$200).

Reports involving death or injury must be filed with the State Boating Law Administrator within 48 hours. Other reports are required within 10 days. Details are available from local U.S. Coast Guard offices.

Supplies

Almost anything, from bubble gum to duct tape, can be used to stop a leak in an emergency. Electrical tape, foam padding from seat cushions, a waterproof vinyl cover and even old rags have been used.

The important thing to do is stuff the material, whatever it is, into the crack or hole with as much pressure as possible. A plugged hole may trickle water but it poses no danger of sinking the vessel except over a long period of time.

One last point to remember: Re-check the leak periodically to be sure that the packing material is still in place.

Going Aground

Going aground can result from operating in shallow water or from leaving your boat on a beach when the tide is going out. The situation is often nothing more than a minor annoyance and an embarrassment since it is usually easy to push the boat off or float it free when the tide rises. Nevertheless, after a grounding you should inspect both the hull and the engine carefully for even minor damage.

WHAT TO DO WHEN YOU RUN AGROUND

1. Shut off the engine immediately.
2. Tilt the drive unit upwards. Check the propeller for damage.
3. Attempt to refloat.
4. Obtain help to refloat.

Check for Damage

If you were under power when you went aground, shift to neutral and shut off the engine immediately to prevent any further damage to the propeller. Check the propeller to see whether it is bent, damaged or broken. To protect the outboard shaft or sterndrive, tilt the drive unit upwards. Examine the hull, inside and out, for leaks or visible damage. If none is found, plan to refloat your boat immediately.

Refloating Yourself

If you are nearly afloat, you may be able to push the boat off. Don't try to restart the engine in shallow water, though, because you may suck sand or gravel into the water intake or damage the propeller.

If the boat is firmly stuck, rocking the boat by having the crew move quickly from side to side may break the suction of a mud or sand bottom. If that doesn't work, it may help to remove weight, including all unneeded crew, so that the boat floats more easily.

If the wind or current is pushing you onto the shore, put an anchor out to seaward to assist in pulling off. The anchor can be floated out on a life cushion by a swimmer and then released. This procedure is called "kedging off." By keeping the anchor line tight, the boat may work itself off naturally. Or you can wait for the incoming tide to pull yourself off.

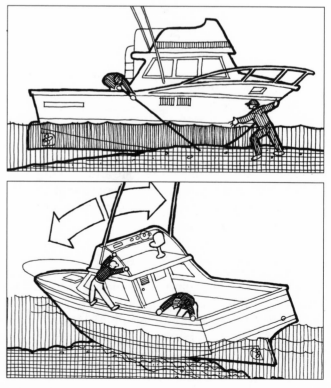

If you are firmly stuck, it may be necesssary to get assistance in refloating your boat after you go aground. If so, there are a couple of techniques to consider before getting started. There are, in addition, legal responsibilities and rights which will affect both you and the owner of the boat rendering assistance to you. This may also influence how you handle the problem.

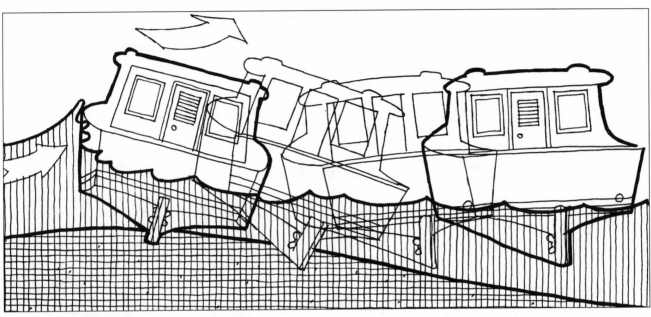

Refloating With Help

One way to get unstuck is to have another powerboat go back and forth nearby, thus creating a wake. As the wake comes in, your boat will float briefly in each surge. Using an anchor to kedge off or simply getting out on the side of the incoming wake and pushing the boat off will move it away from the shore.

LEGAL

There are many misconceptions about Coast Guard duties and salvage rights. The "Good Samaritan" policy has extended to mariners, who will go to each other's assistance as a matter of courtesy and concern without remuneration in mind. However, under strict salvage laws, anyone rendering assistance is entitled to reasonable payment.

If you abandon your boat, it may be claimed by a salvager unless you leave a specific written note saying that you will return. If there is any question, it is best to stay aboard.

If you accept a tow from a commercial towing operator, agree on a price beforehand.

Boatmen are required by law to do everything possible to save lives, but you are not obligated to endanger your crew or your boat to save property.

You may take a tow line from another boat. If you do take a tow, secure it to a strong fitting, such as a towing eye, and protect yourself and your crew in case the line breaks. And be patient. It takes a while for tension on a tow line to pull a boat free.

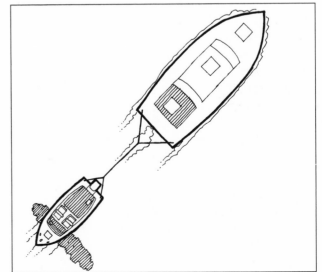

Helping Others/Towing

A fundamental custom of the sea has been for seamen to help each other out of scrapes. Today's skippers still offer assistance to those having problems. This may be as simple as a tow back to the fuel dock or launching ramp, or helping free a boat that's run aground. But both skippers should understand the procedures involved in giving and accepting a tow in order to make the operation go smoothly.

Equipment Needed

The tow line should be sturdy and stretchy. Most boats use their anchor rodes for tow lines. Even if you don't plan to tow far, you may want protection from chafe where the line passes through fittings. Wrap the line with rags or towels. The most effective towing design is a "bridle" on the towing boat, made up of lines of equal length, attached by bowline to a loop at the end of the towed boat's line.

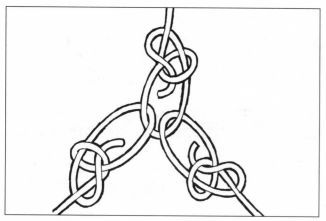

Towing Points

The attachment point must be extremely strong. The bow and stern cleats on modern powerboats are usually designed strongly enough to withstand towing shocks. The bow towing eye or waterski eyes in the stern may be better suited to the task.

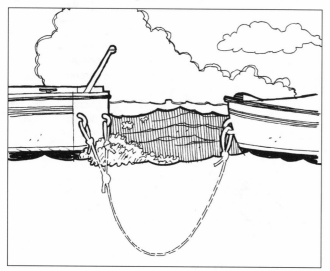

Towing Signals

A VHF radio is the best way to communicate with the other vessel but the universal symbol for "tow line attached securely" is to clasp both hands over your head.

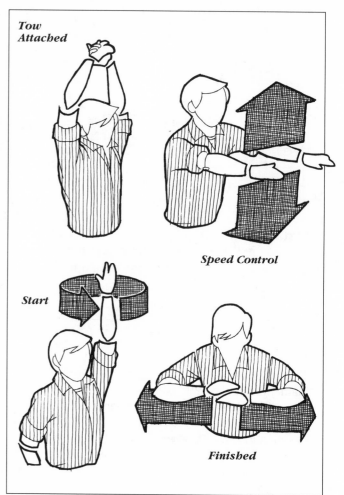

Tow Attached

Speed Control

Start

Finished

Towing Information

It is the responsibility of the towed vessel to indicate how fast to go. Towing a boat too fast can result in loss of control and cause the boat being towed to plow from side to side or to jolt as the boat hits waves. Outboard and sterndrive boats sometimes surge from side to side unless the drive units are raised. If the drive unit can be kept down, you may be able to use it to steer. Try to stay directly behind the towing vessel.

With any luck, you'll never be towed. But you should understand what to expect when you offer someone else a tow. Warn your crew as well as the other crew to stay clear of the tow line when it is under extreme tension. Operate your boat in a cautious manner and you'll have the satisfaction of being a seagoing "Good Samaritan." Remember: Some day you could be at the other end of the tow line.

Passing the Tow Line
Bring your boat close to the other craft and heave the tow line across. Be sure your engine is in neutral until the tow line is clear of your propeller. If the seas are rough and you can't get close enough to throw the line, you can tie it to a buoyant cushion and float it over to the other boat.

Taking Up the Slack
When both ends of the tow line are secured to sturdy fittings and the other crew has signaled that it is ready, idle your boat ahead while a crew member makes sure the tow line is clear. As the line comes taut, slowly increase power to the agreed upon towing speed.

Towing Distance
The longer the tow line, the more it will absorb shocks and be less likely to break. In open water, adjust the tow line so that both boats are on the front face of waves. You don't want to be in the position of trying to pull the other boat "uphill." In harbors, shorten up the tow line for easy maneuvering.

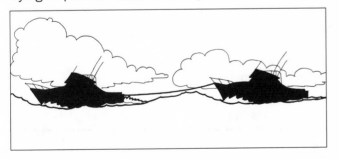

Steering
With the tow line attached to the stern of your boat it will be difficult to steer since the stern will not be free to turn. Leave extra room when making turns. If the towed boat can steer, it should stay in the wake of the tow boat.

LEGAL
The courts have held that the skipper of a boat offering a tow is not legally responsible for damages to the towed vessel so long as the towing skipper "acts as any ordinary, reasonably prudent person would." Although the language is vague, it assumes that the skipper has a level of boating experience acquired with time. If you have any doubts about your own ability to handle a tow, decline the project. You do, however, have a moral (and legal) obligation to save lives. Since you are not responsible for property, you should not get into a situation where you might be accused of damaging property, even if it was done in an honest effort to help. Good seamanship sometimes means standing by until the Coast Guard or some other capable party arrives.

Troubleshooting the Engine

Aboard a small powerboat, the most likely problems you'll encounter will involve the engine. While it seems foolish, your first checkpoint should be the fuel tank to make sure that you actually have fuel. Don't rely on the gas gauge. It may be wrong. Tap the tank or rock the boat to see if you hear fuel sloshing in the tank. If you do have sufficient fuel, try some of the other steps suggested below.

Problem: Starter motor works but engine won't start	
Engine not getting fuel	• Check fuel supply • Make sure fuel valve and fuel tank vent are open • Check fuel line for leaks • Remove and clean fuel filter
Engine flooded	• Let engine sit for 20 minutes with ignition off • Crank engine with throttle fully open (and choke open, if manual) • Try normal starting procedures
Engine overheats	• Allow engine to cool • Check cooling water intake and remove any obstructions • Tighten water pump belt on inboards and check impeller • Check cooling water hoses for leaks • Check oil and refill as needed • Check fresh water cooling tank on inboards and refill
Lack of spark	• Remove wire from one plug, hold it carefully 1/4 inch from engine block, crank engine once. If there is no spark or a pale yellow spark, open the distributor cap and check for corrosion or moisture. A solid blue spark means the ignition is working; test each plug separately.
Fouled spark plugs	• Examine the plugs for carbon or debris and clear the tips • Replace plugs if engine still does not start

Problem: Starter does not operate	
Low battery	• Turn off all lights and allow 30 minutes for battery to recover • Clean battery posts and connections • Check battery cells and fill with fresh water • Tighten alternator belt on inboards

Problem: Engine stops suddenly	
With noise	• Possible damage: broken piston, valve, timing chain
Without noise	• The problem is likely electrical. Inspect wiring and test for spark.
With sputtering and coughing	• The problem is likely fuel. Check for fuel reaching carburetor.

Changing the Propeller

Even the most alert powerboat skipper may occasionally ding the propeller on a floating object or in shallow water. The result may be a small nick in the blade (which can be filed down) or it may bend the entire blade, in which case a spare propeller should be installed. On outboards and sterndrives, this is a simple matter once the drive unit is tilted upwards so that the propeller is accessible above water.

Before starting, lock the tilt mechanism and turn off the ignition so that the drive unit cannot be lowered accidentally.

With pliers, bend the ends of the cotter pin straight and pull it from the hub. Unscrew the hub, being careful to save the thrust washer behind the hub. Remove the damaged propeller, replace the sheer pin where appropriate and insert the new propeller. Replace the thrust washer, screw on the hub snugly and align the hub and shaft holes. Replace the cotter pin and bend back the ends.

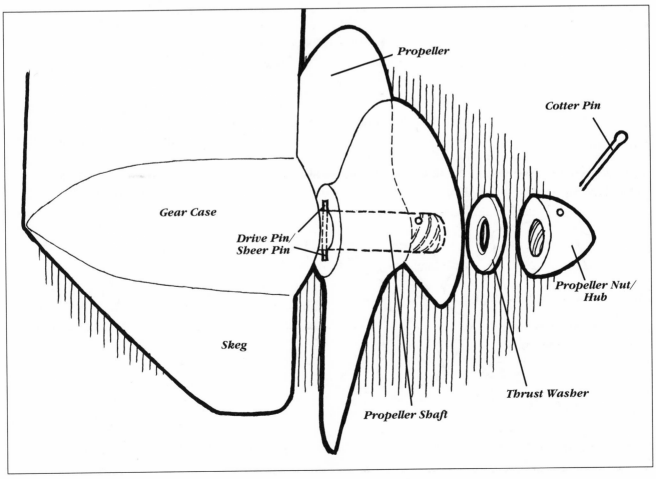

Propeller

Cotter Pin

Gear Case

Drive Pin/
Sheer Pin

Propeller Nut/
Hub

Skeg

Thrust Washer

Propeller Shaft

Troubleshooting a Drive Belt

The drive belts on an inboard or sterndrive engine provide power to the alternator and to the engine's water pump. Both are necessary for the engine to operate. A drive belt may break if it wears, dries and cracks or is not replaced regularly. Constant use in the engine compartment dries out the rubber and causes tiny cracks. You can, however, "jury-rig" a temporary drive belt to get home, if you motor slowly.

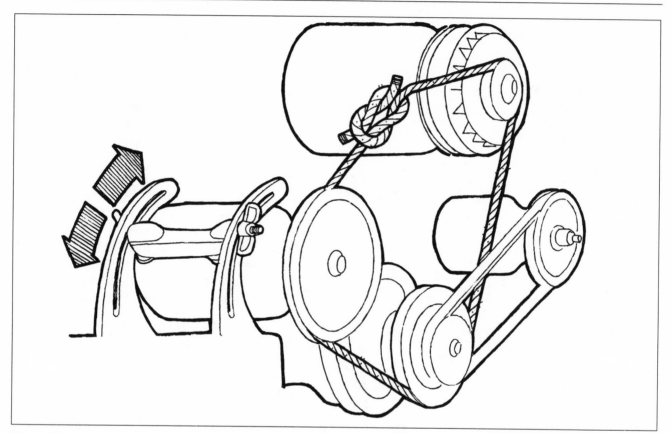

If you do not have a spare drive belt or are unable to install it, you can make a temporary belt out of a length of line. Loosen the adjusting arm next to one of the belt pulleys. Tie the line around the pulleys and secure it with a square knot. Trim off the excess line that may snag. Tighten the adjusting arm for maximum tension. The temporary repair will wear and slip but it may help to get you back. Check it regularly to make sure that it hasn't broken or slipped off, and run the engine at low speed only.

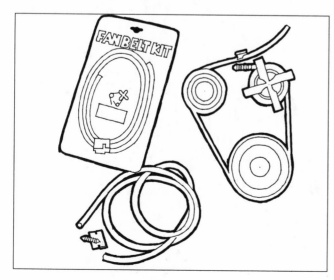

Emergency fan belt kits, available at auto parts stores, consist of a length of tubing and connector. Cut the tubing to the desired length and connect it. The belt is a "get home" device designed to help avoid towing costs.

Emergency Steering

The steering system on most modern powerboats consists of hydraulics, levers and cables. Although a broken steering system is rare, the inability to use the wheel to steer will not prevent you from returning to port as long as the engine is running. You can improvise substitute steering systems using on-board gear that will enable you to get home, not quickly but not at the end of a tow line either.

Disconnecting the Outboard

Many outboards have a quick-release fitting for the steering system that allows you to remove the frozen steering system and steer the boat by turning the engine by hand. Because there's powerful torque involved, lash a paddle along the side of the outboard to act as a tiller. With this kind of jury rig you cannot go too fast.

Steering With a Paddle

You can experiment using your paddle or a water-ski as a makeshift rudder. With the engine at idle speed, you can drag the paddle on one side of the boat to make it turn in that direction. If you find that the boat wants to continue straight, put the engine in neutral, swing the boat to a new course with the paddle, then put the engine in gear again.

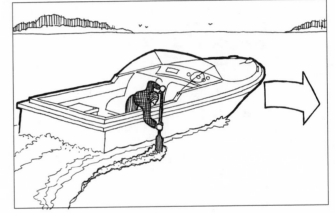

Steering With a Drogue

A drogue is any bulky object dragged through the water astern. It can be a thick coil of line, a small but sturdy bucket or even a fender with anchor chain attached for weight. Make a bridle from two pieces of line and loop them twice around the cleats on each corner of the stern. With the drogue directly behind the boat, you will go straight. When the line on one side is eased, the drogue will move off center and the boat will move in the drogue's direction. It will take effort to re-center the drogue after each change. Remember to keep the bridle clear of the propeller.

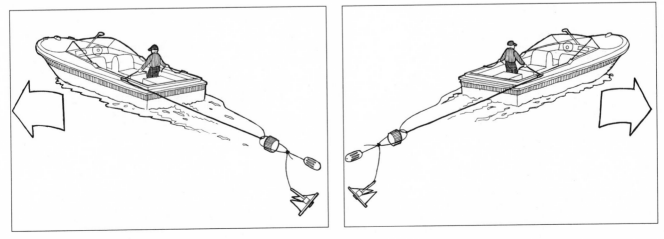

Mechanical Solutions

Electricity and water, particularly salt water, can prove to be a breeding ground for irritating problems that range from a seemingly dead engine to cabin lights that flicker on and off. Preventive maintenance is the best way to keep your electrical system operating with all the lights burning. When problems do occur, however, a methodical troubleshooting program is the easiest way to set things right again.

The Batteries
Each cell should be filled with distilled water to the "split ring." The top of the battery and the battery posts should be clean and free of corrosion. If the cable clamps or posts need cleaning, a mild solution of baking soda and water will neutralize the acids. The same solution can be used on the top of the battery but be sure it doesn't get into the cells themselves.

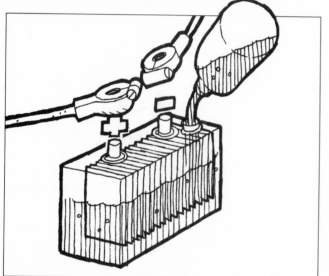

The Master Switch
This is often a four position switch: Off, Batt 1, Both, Batt 2. If your lights work erratically, try moving the switch handle slightly to see if you get better contact off center.

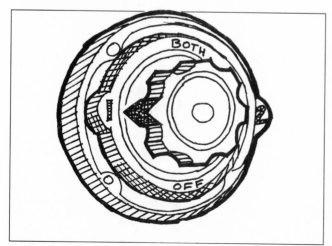

Circuit Breakers
Most powerboats now use circuit breakers rather than fuses for their electrical systems. If you have problems with a particular circuit, try jiggling the breaker slightly. If this does not work, the breaker itself may be faulty.

Wiring
It's not hard to trace the wiring from a particular circuit on a small boat since most wiring is now color coded. Look for breaks or worn spots where the wire passes through bulkheads or around corners. Replace the wire or tape the break.

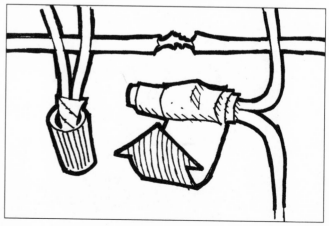

Chapter 6

Captains Courageous

Night Boating

You are required to turn on your navigation lights at sunset for three reasons. First, they announce your presence to others. Second, the lights on your boat tell a lot about its size and the kind of work it's engaged in. Third, navigation lights tell you in which direction a boat is traveling. You are most apt to encounter the running lights shown below. For a complete listing, see *Chapman Piloting*.

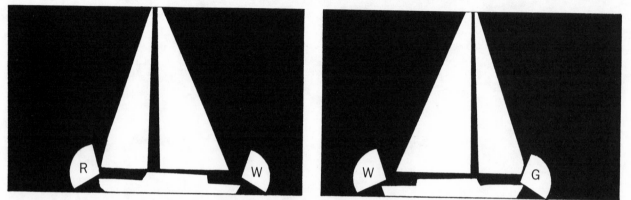

Sailboat Above 23 Feet

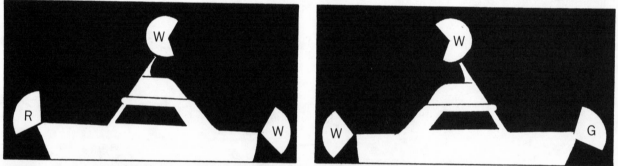

Powerboat Under 39 Feet

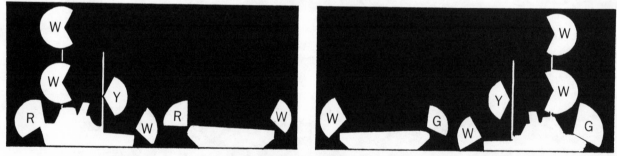

Vessel in Tow

Large Power Vessel

Lighted Buoys

Lighted navigational buoys have their own individual light codes which allow them to be identified and located on a chart. Both the color and the rhythm of the flash are distinctive, enabling you to easily determine your exact position on the water and navigate safely through channels. The buoys listed on this page are representative, not comprehensive. See *Chapman Piloting* for a complete listing.

BUOYS ON CHARTS
Buoys are indicated by slanted diamonds located over a circle. The light is indicated below the buoy number. "Fl G 6sec" means a flashing green light of six-second duration. Example:

LIGHT PERIOD
The period of a light is the time it takes to complete one full cycle of light and dark periods. A "Flashing 6 seconds" light takes six seconds before the sequence is repeated. Standard light periods are 2.5, 4 and 6 seconds.

LIGHT COLORS
Red Lights mark the starboard side of a channel when entering from seaward or when proceeding upstream. They also mark hazards to pass with the buoy to starboard.

Green Lights indicate the port side of a channel when entering from seaward, as well as hazards to keep on your port side.

White Lights are used to indicate the middle of the channel.

LIGHT RHYTHMS
The lights on buoys and beacons flash in five patterns to separate them from background lights as well as to help identify and locate them on your charts.

Fixed Lights: A steady light, shown on charts as "F."

Flashing Lights: A single brief flash at regular intervals. The flash is always less than the interval of darkness. When green or red colors are used to mark the port or starboard side of a channel. Shown on charts as "Fl."
Flash sequence:

Quick Flashing Lights: These flash at least 60 times each minute, and are used to indicate areas of special caution. This rhythm is being phased out. Shown on

older charts as "Qk Fl"; on new charts as "Q."
Flash sequence:

Occulting Lights: These differ from flashing lights because the period of light is longer than the period of darkness. Shown on charts as "Occ" plus the darkness interval between flashes.
Flash sequence:

Isophase Lights: These flash with equal periods of dark and light. Shown on charts as "Iso."
Flash sequence:

Composite Group Flashing Lights (2+1): These are typified by two brief flashes, a short dark interval, a single brief flash, and then several seconds of darkness. Used to mark channel junctions that can be passed on either side. Shown on charts as "Fl(2+1)."
Flash sequence:

Morse Code "A" Flashing Lights: Always white, these lights are the dot-dash of the Morse code letter "A." A short flash and a brief dark period are followed by a longer flash and longer dark period, repeated every eight seconds. Used as mid-channel lights. Shown on charts as "Mo(A)."
Flash sequence:

Sound Signals

Sound is used to signal intent or action between vessels. While the Inland Rules and the International Rules are generally similar, sound signals under Inland Rules for head-on, crossing and overtaking situations are signals of intent, whereas under International Rules they signal an action taking place. The most common Inland signals are illustrated below. For a complete listing, see *Chapman Piloting*.

Terms

Short Blast: A blast of one second duration ●

Prolonged Blast: A blast of four to six seconds ⬬

Restricted Visibility: Rules that apply to vessels not in sight of each each other when navigating in or near an area of restricted visibility (Inland and International Rules are identical).

Signals to Attract Attention: Any sound signal or combination that cannot be mistaken for any signal authorized anywhere else in the rules.

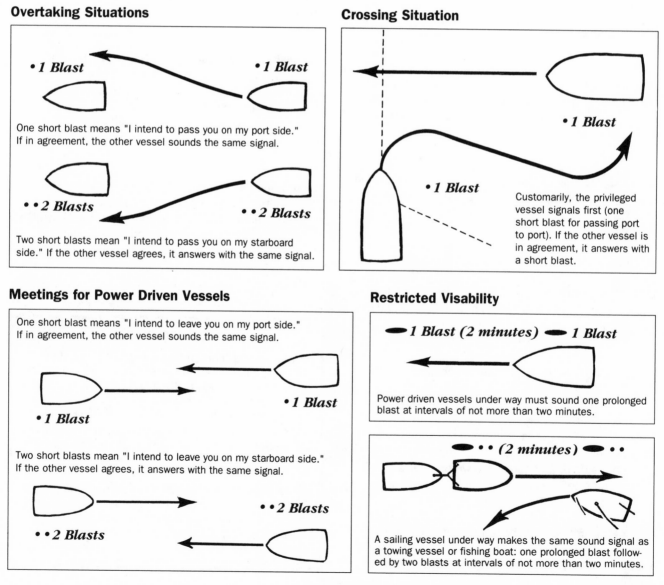

Overtaking Situations

• 1 Blast   **• 1 Blast**

One short blast means "I intend to pass you on my port side." If in agreement, the other vessel sounds the same signal.

• • 2 Blasts   **• • 2 Blasts**

Two short blasts mean "I intend to pass you on my starboard side." If the other vessel agrees, it answers with the same signal.

Crossing Situation

• 1 Blast

• 1 Blast

Customarily, the privileged vessel signals first (one short blast for passing port to port). If the other vessel is in agreement, it answers with a short blast.

Meetings for Power Driven Vessels

One short blast means "I intend to leave you on my port side." If in agreement, the other vessel sounds the same signal.

• 1 Blast   **• 1 Blast**

Two short blasts mean "I intend to leave you on my starboard side." If the other vessel agrees, it answers with the same signal.

• • 2 Blasts   **• • 2 Blasts**

Restricted Visability

⬬ 1 Blast (2 minutes) ⬬ 1 Blast

Power driven vessels under way must sound one prolonged blast at intervals of not more than two minutes.

⬬ • • (2 minutes) ⬬ • •

A sailing vessel under way makes the same sound signal as a towing vessel or fishing boat: one prolonged blast followed by two blasts at intervals of not more than two minutes.

Inlet Running

An inlet can be difficult to enter when tide and harbor shallows cause waves to start breaking in the entrance. The waves can sometimes be dangerous and, unless there is an urgent reason to get to shore, it is safer to wait outside for smoother water to develop when the tide changes. It also stands to reason that when leaving the harbor, it is best to wait until the waves in the inlet have subsided.

Assessing the Inlet: If you aren't familiar with the inlet, watch other boats pass through the waves. Study the wave pattern. There is often a series of three or five waves followed by a small wave, which is what you want for your entrance.

Preparing the Boat: If you are concerned about conditions, have your crew put on life jackets, close hatches and center crew weight slightly aft to keep the bow up.

Entering the Inlet: Since it is important to keep your boat lined up with the waves, you should be prepared to steer quickly. Watch the waves both ahead and behind you. The safest place to be is on the back side of an incoming wave. Adjust your speed to stay ahead of the wave behind you but don't go so fast that you catch up with the crest ahead. Some fast powerboats, such as the one shown below, will be able to ride the top of the crest safely.

Heavy Weather Seamanship

Most modern powerboats are designed to handle bad weather in reasonable comfort, whether it's wind from an offshore blow or a summer squall on a lake. It is up to the skipper to know how to steer a course that will be dry and safe, as well as comfortable in adverse circumstances. This requires being thoroughly familiar with your boat and developing the following techniques on rough or stormy waters.

Foul Weather Seamanship
Prepare for rough conditions by closing all hatches and securing all portholes. Loose objects, particularly anything heavy or sharp, should be stored securely or tied down so that they can't cause any damage or injury.

Heading into Large Seas
Speed is a critical factor in these conditions. A setting just below planing speed is usually the most comfortable, allowing your boat to cross the tops of waves and drop into the troughs gently. Keep your hand on the throttle and keep adjusting speed to individual wave conditions.

In some cases, quartering the waves is more satisfactory, which means steering so that the boat is going into the waves at an angle rather than perpendicular to them.

Steering Parallel to Waves
This is likely to be an uncomfortable and not very safe ride because you'll be rolling with the waves. It may be wet from spray as well. A better plan is to zigzag toward your destination, quartering into the waves for a while and then running with them so that your boat rides more easily.

A powerboat's square stern puts it at a disadvantage when running before large waves. A large sea can push the boat forward into the wave trough or can push it sideways down a wave. Turning a small powerboat around in large waves can also be tricky unless it is done in a trough. Fortunately there are seamanlike ways for powerboat skippers to handle both situations in stormy weather.

Running Before the Waves

In large waves, particularly those that are breaking occasionally, it is important to maintain enough speed to stay ahead of the crests. The ideal position for a small powerboat is on the back side of the wave ahead, with the skipper adjusting the boat's speed to maintain this ride. If your boat is not fast enough to stay with the waves, try quartering down the face of the waves to present a corner of your stern to the crest rather than the flat transom. Use power to control any tendency to turn sideways.

Turning Around in Waves

If you decide you want to change direction, execute the turn as quickly as possible at the bottom of the trough or on the back of the preceding wave. That will give you time to set the boat to go straight up the crest or gain enough speed to stay on top of the wave if you have turned it to run with the seas.

Courses and Organizations

Several non-profit organizations offer boating courses, instructional material and services of interest to owners and operators of small powerboats. Most courses and printed material are free for the asking, and can be helpful for the novice skipper and seasoned owner alike. Safe boating courses are also taught at local schools as well as city and state government agencies.

United States Coast Guard
The USCG Office of Boating Safety produces many informative pamphlets and films about small boat handling. These are available from the local USCG District Headquarters or from the Coast Guard Auxiliary.

United States Coast Guard Auxiliary Washington, D.C., 20593. This civilian organization conducts boating classes, patrols the waterways and conducts courtesy boat examinations. The Auxiliary in your area can be contacted through the Coast Guard District Headquarters.

United States Power Squadrons P.O. Box 30423, Raleigh, NC 27622. This volunteer organization conducts a series of free basic introductory courses. Call (800) 336-BOAT for information on the USPS courses that are available in your area.

American Red Cross
With more than 2,800 chapters in the U.S., the Red Cross is noted for its first aid, CPR and water safety courses, including a small craft safety course. In addition, the organization publishes books and pamphlets on boating and water safety. Contact the Red Cross through its local office.

National Oceanic and Atmospheric Administration (NOAA)
A division of NOAA, the National Weather Service, produces many pamphlets of interest to boatowners on boating weather topics, which are available from the U.S. Government Printing Office, Washington, D.C., 20402 or from local NWS offices.

In addition, the U.S. Army Corps of Engineers, the National Park Service and National State Boating Law Administrators publish information concerning boating on waterways in their jurisdictions.

Further Reading

Boating is a sport where the learning process will continue as you become interested in different aspects of boat operation, navigation, cruising and repairs. The best way to learn new skills is aboard your boat, but books can provide a good addition to personal experience. Besides the books listed below, there are a number of national and regional boating publications available to further hone your seamanship.

Advanced First Aid Afloat, by Dr. Peter F. Eastman (Cornell Maritime Press). Comprehensive, with lists of suggested supplies to have onboard.

Boatkeeper, ed. by Bernard Gladstone and Tom Bottomley (Wm. Morrow & Co.). The how-to, where-to and what-to of marine maintenance.

Boatman's Handbook, by Tom Bottomley (Wm. Morrow & Co.). A handy, easy-to-use take-aboard book.

Chapman Piloting, Seamanship & Small Boat Handling, by Elbert S. Maloney (Wm. Morrow & Co.). The indispensable boating reference recommended by U.S. Power Squadrons and the U.S. Coast Guard Auxiliary.

The Complete Book of Anchoring and Mooring, by Earl Hinz (Cornell Maritime Press). Though directed toward cruising yachts, it has good information for small powerboats.

Contingency Seamanship, by John Clemens (Ziff-Davis). Help in coping with the unexpected at sea.

Cooking on the Go, by Janet Groene (Wm. Morrow & Co.). An invaluable cookbook and guide to provisioning.

Dutton's Navigation & Piloting, by Elbert S. Maloney (Naval Institute Press). A concise navigation manual.

Eldridge Tide and Pilot Book (Robert Eldridge White). A comprehensive list of tide and current tables and other valuable marine information.

The Guide to High Performance Powerboating, by Joanne A. Fishman (Wm. Morrow & Co.). The definitive guide to buying, maintaining and achieving peak performance.

An Introduction to Powerboat Cruising, by Dag Pike (Wm. Morrow & Co.). A popular introduction to buying, owning and operating a powerboat.

Knight's Modern Seamanship, by John Noel (Van Nostrand Reinhold). Provides authoritative answers to a wide range of questions about boats.

The Morrow Guide to Knots, by Mario Bigon and Guido Regazzoni (Wm. Morrow & Co.). A how-to guide to a wide selection of knots, hitches and loops.

The Motor Cruising Manual, by John Mellor (David & Charles). Good information on small powerboat cruising.

Navigation Rules, International-Inland (U.S. Coast Guard). Listing of official navigation rules and regulations governing all vessels afloat.

Stapleton's Powerboat Bible, by Sid Stapleton (Wm. Morrow & Co.). How to buy, equip and organize a boat for coastal and bluewater cruising.

Time-Life Library of Boating (Time-Life Books). A 12-volume set of well-researched and illustrated boating books.

United States Power Squadrons' Boating Course Video and Booklet (Wm. Morrow & Co.). You can now earn your basic boating certificate from the first video edition of the nationally recognized USPS course.

The Yachtman's Emergency Handbook, by Neil Hollander and Harald Mertes (Wm. Morrow & Co.). Over 500 procedures for all emergency situations.

Your Boat Belowdecks, by Thomas Reale and Michael Johnson (Wm. Morrow & Co.). A much-needed how-to repair manual.

Your Boat's Electrical System, by Conrad Miller and Elbert S. Maloney (Wm. Morrow & Co.). Discusses at the practical level every circuit used aboard a boat.

Dictionary and Index

Nothing has influenced the English language as much as the nautical world. We launch a business, ship a package and board a train. When an undertaking is effortless, it is smooth sailing. When depressed, we're in the doldrums. Or we may be told to shape up or ship out. We are eager to hear the latest scuttlebutt, back a friend to the bitter end and scorn the big wigs that run things—all terms from the sea.

Abaft: Behind

Abeam: At right angles to a boat (p. 10)

Aboard: On a boat

Adrift: Unsecured

Aft: Toward the stern (p. 10)

Aground: Stuck on the bottom in shallow water

Aid to Navigation: A buoy, lighthouse or other marker shown on charts (p. 50)

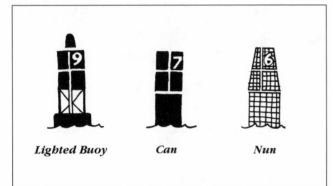

Lighted Buoy   *Can*   *Nun*

Alongside: Beside

Amidship(s): The middle of a boat

Anchor: A device used to secure the boat to the bottom using a line called a rode (p. 78)

Anchor Light: A white light displayed at night while the boat is anchored (p. 11)

Backfire Flame Arrestor: A filter over the engine carburetor to prevent fire in the engine compartment (p. 27)

Bail: To remove water from a boat

Beam: The widest point of a boat (p. 10)

Below: In the cabin or beneath the deck

Bilge: The lowest inside point in the boat

Bilge Blower: A Coast Guard-required electrically operated fan for supplying fresh air to and exhaust fumes from the engine compartment (p. 11)

Bilge Pump: A manual or electric water pump used to remove water from the lowest part of the boat (p. 98)

Bimini Top: A fabric sunshade over the helm station that can be folded down (p. 29)

Boarding Ladder: A set of steps for getting in or out of the water (p. 12)

Boathook: A pole with a hook on the end (p. 12)

Boat Supports: Rollers or carpeted planks on a trailer to cradle the boat (p. 24)

Bow: The most forward part of a boat (p. 10)

Bow Eye: A metal fitting just above the waterline on the bow, used to attach the trailer winch cable or for towing the boat on the water (p. 56)

Bowline: An easily untied knot that is used for making a loop (p. 82)

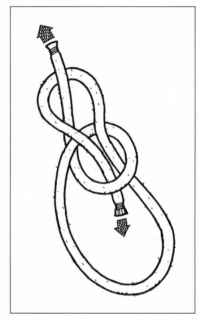

Bowrail: A grabrail around the front of the boat (p. 11)

Bowrider: A boat with a seating area forward of the windshield (p. 14)

Bulkhead: A wall in the cabin (p. 10)

Bungee: A shock cord with hooks at each end, used for storage (p. 85)

Burdened Vessel: Vessel which must keep out of the way of privileged vessel (p. 42)

Buoy: A floating marker in a channel (p. 52)

Capacity Plate: A required plate that displays maximum capacities and horsepower for a boat (p. 11)

Cast Off: To release a line

Center Console: A boat whose steering console is surrounded by a walk-around cockpit (p. 14)

A "scuttlebutt" aboard a sailing ship was the water cask (with a scuttle for drinking) and the crew gathered around to gossip, just as businesspeople do by the office water cooler. The bitter end is the end of an important line and, when you've reached it, you're probably in big trouble. Big wigs were the senior Royal Navy officers who wore huge wigs when in command of a sailing ship.

Chafe: Abrasion on a line

Channel: Water deep enough for boating

Chart: A nautical map (p. 50)

Chock: A fitting that prevents chafe (p. 12)

Chop: Short, steep waves

Cleat: An object to which lines are secured (p. 12)

Clove Hitch: A knot used to hold constant loads such as dock lines (p. 82)

Cockpit: A recessed area where the crew sits (p. 10)

Coil: To organize a line in loops for storage (p. 83)

Compass: A navigational instrument that indicates magnetic north (p. 12)

Compass Rose: The circle on a chart showing magnetic and true bearings (p. 72)

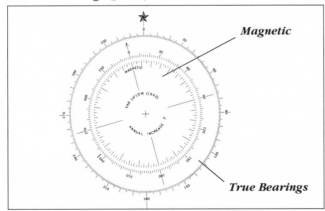

Magnetic

True Bearings

Control Panel: The instrument panel on a boat

Cotter Pin: A small pin used to keep the propeller in place (p. 111)

Course: The compass direction that is steered

Cuddy Cabin: A small cabin that usually contains bunks and a head (p. 15)

Current: Movement of the water caused by tide or wind

Dead Reckoning: The calculation of a boat's position using speed, time, previous position, recent course and current or drift

Deck: The top of a hull (p. 10)

Depth Sounder: A navigation and safety device that indicates water depth (p. 91)

Dividers: An instrument used for measuring distance on a chart (p. 73)

Dock Lines: Pieces of rope intended to tie the boat to the dock (p. 12)

Doglegs: Changes in course to clear obstacles

Drain Plugs: Rubber and metal fittings used to seal drain holes in the hull (p. 32)

Drive Unit: The portion of a sterndrive outside the boat, including the propeller and housing (p. 17)

Drogue: Any bulky object dragged through the water astern (p. 113)

Ebb: The outgoing tide

Engine Cover: On an inboard or sterndrive boat, an enclosure over the engine (p. 11)

Eye: A loop in a line

Fender: A rubber object intended to protect the hull from docks and other boats (p. 12)

Fend Off: To push away

Flagstaff: A pole on the stern for attaching a flag (p. 12)

Float Plan: An intended itinerary and schedule (p. 33)

Foredeck: The covered deck area at the bow (p. 10)

Forward: Toward the bow (p. 10)

Freeboard: The vertical distance between the waterline and the deck

Fuel Filler: The opening in the deck that leads to the gas tank (p. 11)

Fuel Line: The metal or rubber hose that carries fuel to the engine from the tank

Galley: A boat kitchen

Gear: General term for all equipment on a boat

Gearshift/Throttle: Controls near the helm for speed and direction (p. 11)

Grabrails: Low railings used as handholds on the deck or around the cockpit (p. 12)

Dictionary and Index

Starboard, the nautical right side of a boat, came from the Norsemen, who steered their boats not with a rudder but with a paddle over the right side of the boat. This was called the "steerboard," which was corrupted to starboard. Naturally, because the steering gear was on the right side and could be damaged by a pier, the left side of a boat was put nearest the shore, thus becoming known as the "port" side.

Half-hitch: A knot used to secure lines that may shift in direction (p. 82)

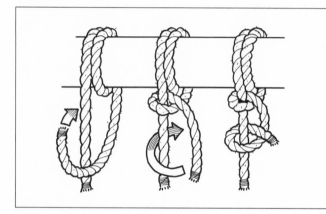

Hatch: An opening in the deck for light and ventilation (p. 10)

Head: A boat bathroom (p. 11)

Heave: To throw

Heel: To tip a boat sideways (p. 106)

Helm: The steering wheel (p. 11)

Helm Station: Where the steering wheel and engine controls are located

Hitch: The ball-shaped attachment point on a car for towing a boat (p. 24)

Horn: Used to warn others of your presence and to signal your intentions (p. 11)

Hull: The body of a boat (p. 16)

Inlet: An entry to a harbor from the ocean (p. 119)

Inboard: An engine that drives the boat via a propeller shaft through the bottom of the hull (p. 17)

Jetdrive: A boat propelled by a high-pressure stream of water from an engine-operated pump (p. 17)

Jury Rig: To improvise a replacement

Kedge Off: To use an anchor to pull a grounded boat free (p. 106)

Knot: One nautical mile per hour

Landmark: A recognizable object on shore

Launch: To move a boat from shore to water (p. 34)

Leeward: The side of the boat opposite the wine or direction the wind is blowing towards

Line: A length of rope

Loran: An electronic navigation instrument used for finding your boat's position, an acronym for Long Range Navigation (p. 75)

Markers: Lobster pot buoys (p. 47)

Nautical Mile: The unit of distance used on nautical charts, equal to 6,076 feet, or 1.15 statute miles. A statue mile equals .87 nautical mile.

Navigation Lights: Lights required on boats for night operation (p. 11)

Outboard: A self-contained engine and drive system that clamps on the transom (p. 17)

Outdrive: The underwater propulsion unit for a sterndrive boat (p. 11)

Overhead: A ceiling on a boat

Overtaking: Coming up from astern and passing

Parallel Rules: A navigation instrument used for transferring a course to or from a compass rose (p. 72)

PFD: Personal Flotation Device, or life jacket (p. 28)

Pier: A fixed platform that extends from shore

Pilings: Wood or concrete posts driven into the seabed for mooring boats or piers (p. 36)

Piloting: Navigation within sight of land

Plot: To set a course on a chart

Port: The left side of a boat when facing forward, or a window (p. 10)

Privileged Vessel: Vessel with the right of way (p. 42)

Prop: The propeller (p. 11)

Reef: An underwater hazard of shallow water

Right of Way: The legal right to remain on the present course (p. 42)

Rode: The anchor line (p. 49)

Rod Holder: A recessed fitting that holds fishing rods ready for use

Rubrail: A metal or rubber railing around the deck that protects the hull (p. 11)

Rudder: An underwater steering device

Runabout: A general term for small open cockpit powerboats (p. 14)

Youngsters the world over know that they should "mind their p's and q's," but the phrase comes from drunken sailors and not bad children. Sailors were given credit in waterfront taverns where the innkeeper marked drinks on a chalkboard. A wise sailor knew enough to carefully watch the innkeeper mark his "pints" and "quarts" so that he wouldn't be overcharged as the evening progressed.

Running Lights: The lights used by boats under way between sundown and sunup

Safe Speed: Speed taking into consideration visibility and obstructions in the area (p. 42)

Scope: The ratio between the anchor rode let out to the water depth

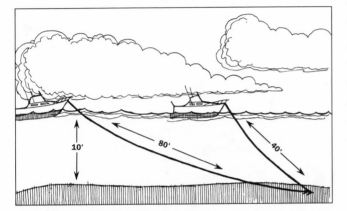

Seabags: Soft fabric bags used instead of suitcases on boats (p. 30)

Seacock: A valve through the hull (p. 105)

Secure: To fasten a line to a cleat or fitting

Shackle: A metal fitting that secures one piece of equipment to another

Skipper: The person in charge of a boat

Slip: An assigned docking area (p. 55)

Sole: A floor on a boat

Squall: A sudden local storm

Stacking: A method of storing boats in enclosed racks that saves space (p. 23)

Stakes: Fishing nets (p. 47)

Starboard: The right-hand side of a boat when facing forward (p. 10)

Stern: The back part of the boat (p. 10)

Sterndrive: A propulsion system with the engine inside the hull and a drive unit attached to the outside of the transom (p. 17)

Stern Light: A white navigation light mounted at the stern of a boat (p. 11)

Strakes: On a fiberglass hull, the longitudinal ridges on the underwater surface used to reduce spray and improve stability (p. 13)

Stringers: Heavy beams of wood or fiberglass running fore and aft inside the hull, used to support the flooring and engines (p. 16)

Sway Bars: Bars attached to the rear suspension of a tow car to stiffen and control the handling (p. 25)

Tachometer: A gauge on the control panel that indicates engine revolutions (p. 74)

Tide: The rise and fall of water in the ocean

Tie-Downs: Ropes or straps used to secure a boat to a trailer (p. 24)

Tongue: The main beam of a trailer that connects to the automobile (p. 25)

Tonneau Cover: A snap-on cover used to protect unused areas of a boat against sun and rain

Transom: The outer surface of the stern (p. 10)

Troubleshooting: The methodical solution to mechanical problems

Turk's Head: An ornate knot used for decoration

Upwind: The direction from which the wind blows

Ventilator Ducts: Scoops used to vent fresh air into or from a boat hull

Vessel: Any boat or ship

VHF/FM: A Very High Frequency radio telephone

Visual Distress Signal: A governmental term for flares, signal flags, mirrors or other methods of attracting attention (p. 27)

Wake: The turbulence left behind a moving boat (p. 46)

Waterline: The line around the hull that marks where the boat floats at rest (p. 10)

Weight Capacity Plate: A plate on a trailer listing the maximum acceptable load and tire size (p. 25)

Winch: An electric or manual drum for pulling a boat onto a trailer (p. 25)

Windward: The side of the boat or direction the wind is blowing from

WX: A symbol, used on VHF radios and elsewhere, for the weather

ART CREDITS:

James E. Mitchell
Pages 7, 8, 9, 20, 21, 23, 30, 31, 34, 35, 36, 37, 38, 39, 40, 41, 42, 43, 44, 45, 54, 55, 56, 57, 61, 62, 63, 64, 65, 66, 67, 68, 69, 70, 71, 79, 80, 81, 115, 117, 119, 120, 121, 123, 128

Lawrence Jan Zwart
Pages 10, 11, 12, 13, 14, 15, 16, 17, 24, 25, 26, 27, 28, 29, 32, 46, 47, 48, 49, 50, 51, 52, 53, 58, 59, 60, 70, 72, 73, 74, 75, 76, 77, 78, 82, 83, 84, 85, 86, 87, 88, 89, 90, 91, 92, 93, 94, 95, 96, 97, 98, 99, 100, 101, 102, 103, 104, 105, 106, 107, 108, 109, 111, 112, 113, 114, 118, 124, 125, 126, 127

PREPARED FOR HEARST MARINE BOOKS BY PRESTIGE PUBLICATIONS, INC., NEW YORK

Editor - Reginald Bragonier, Jr.
Art Director - Shelley Heller
Associate Editor - Kate Krader
Assistant Editors - Mary Justin, Sharon McLaughlin

The editors gratefully acknowledge the assistance of Dan Fales, Executive Editor, Motorboating & Sailing.